THE TREE

AN ANIMAL FABLE

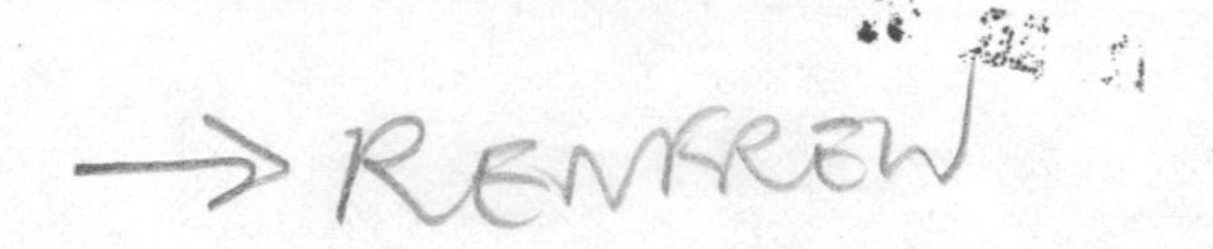

Tom Scott

BORDERLINE PRESS
Dunfermline
1977

Published by BORDERLINE PRESS
96 Halbeath Road, Dunfermline.

Cover by Gordon Stewart.

ISBN 0 906135 00 1.

Extracts from *The Tree* have appeared in the following periodicals: Chapman, Littack and Scotia Review.

Printed by John McKinlay,
11-15 King Street, Perth, Scotland.

For Heather,

with love and thanks.

Storys to rede ar delitabill
Suppois that thae be nocht but fabill:
Then suld storys that suthfast wer ...
Have doubill plesance in heryng ...
Tharfor I wald fayne set my will
Giff my wyt mycht suffice thartill,
To put in wryt a suthfast story ...

(John Barbour, *The Brus,* 1375)

The great tree of life which fills with its dead and broken branches the crust of the earth, and covers the surface with its ever-branching and beautiful ramifications.

(Charles Darwin)

We want the creative faculty to imagine that which we know ... we want the poetry of life.

(Percy Bysshe Shelley)

I think that I shall never see
A poem lovely as a tree ...

(Joyce Kilmer)

And the author offers up a prayer of thanks for the life of a certain ninth century Irishman famous to the world of thought as Johannes Scotus Erigena – that is to say, John the Irish-born Scot, whose *Of the Divisions of Nature* gave him the first glimpse of this Tree.

AUTHOR'S NOTE

Although this is a poetic work, not a scientific, my debt (though not uncritical) to Darwin and all scholarship in a field I knew as 'Nature Study' in boyhood is vast and obvious, my gratitude correspondingly great. But my interest was and is aesthetic, not scientific. I paraphrase that great pioneer of ocean exploration, Jacques Cousteau, in saying that a fact is an emotional thing, that one cannot separate facts from what we feel about them. Facts therefore are poetic things, material of poetry. This has always been true and the only difference between my Polysemous Veritism and previous poetry is only of degree, not kind: but this art is to our time what Polysemous Allegory was to Dante's.

The versification might best be described as post-Hopkins heroic verse, and I call it symphonic verse. Its debt to so-called 'blank' verse is obvious: but it owes even more to the old Anglo-Saxon alliterative line. As in that line, and in Hopkins Sprung Rhythm, the stresses are regular (normally five to the line), the non-stress syllables irregular. I had in mind a bar as in music, in which you can have two full notes to the bar, one and two-halves, or one and a triplet, or one and four quarters, thus: Taa taa; taa tate; taa tatefi; taa tafatifi. In other words the unstressed syllables may be one, two in the time of one, three or four in the time of one, without losing the basic bar pattern. Rarely I have six stresses to a line; even more rarely only four or three.

The problem of gender: to avoid using his or her where both or either is meant, I have invented a form 'hir' (his/her): and for he-or-she, a form 'heor'. But I try to avoid the problem as much as I can, lest the reader is irritated.

I owe an immense debt of gratitude to Joy M. Hendry, without whose selfless and expert labours this work might have been born only to blush unseen.

1

(1)

Not even the rocks can tell it all, the tale
of how our Mother Earth sprang from the Sun
to anchor in her orbit round her lord,
one in a Muses' nonead of planets:
but rumours reach us, hints are handed down
from learned man to learned, till at last
as may a mighty ship loom up through fog
or some dew-dank mountain to a seaman's eye
shoulder at dawn through shrouds of ocean night,
so loom up some limbs of our tree, our fable.

Out of the heart of mystery we come
into the heart of mystery pilgrimming on,
our knowledge charting but unknowable seas,
skin-deep sketching of unfathomable ocean
of space and time, of length, breadth and thickness.
For we, animal beings, beings with souls,
in logic's trammels can no more take life
than lunatics in trawls can net the moon.

Yet say our Mother Earth in our Sun's embrace
conceived, gestated in some billions years
(time to her no time but eternity)
brought together in breeding ocean atoms
in molecules, in various compounds, acids,
proteins, fats and enzymes, bore them into
the light, and life was born, the single cell,
(Darwin's one and only Ancestor?)
each a solar system in microgram,
its nucleus a planet-haremed sun –
cosmos in a cent of a grain of sand.

Out of mystery issued the simple soul
into a steamy wonder-world of water,
spawn-thick life-stuff, gluey in every airt,
till here and there and (who knows?) everywhere
of that prime plasm the first species formed,
came in millions, meek inheritors,
from eight inanimate elements animate matter

came, matter with soul, organic life
in some mysterious alchemy composed,
beings of purpose, identity, free will,
beings that breathe and move, digest, excrete,
constrained by hard necessity to choose,
reject, respond to stimuli, stay alive,
adapt, and by dividing multiply,
planting seed in the vegetable ocean fields,
self food-factories by self roots gristed.

Came in this ocean garden of Eden the fall,
the failed plant (some factory failure) forced
by inexorable law to prey on others:
and so plant-eating animal life was born,
born to prey, and to be preyed upon,
establishing a neotenic law —
not only the meek but the weak inherit Earth,
for deviation mothers invention's mother
and grandmothers man as ape that couldn't grow up:
so if Man forfeit his consulship of Earth,
no whale succeeds but likely some weaker form.

Dependent on plants, themselves on Earth dependent,
we, the animals, were born; and if
from some stuck halfling sprouting seraph wings
an angel kingdom comes, they too will prey
unless they bring some law as yet unknown.
For us, that fall into our predator guilt
the first step took on the road to Calvary
and our holy prey consumed in Eucharist,
flesh and blood of the victim Nazarene.

But first these first (and last?) of animals
who've seen millions of years of mighty lizards
come, and go millions of years ago,
who fare to outlast us at least as long:
our countless parent, sperm of all zoa
(not some mythical one pan-ancestor).
For, as our Sun sucks water up in clouds
and showers it down upon the land as rain
that trickles and gathers in little rills and streamlets

countless as the plankton in the sea,
merging into streams that merge into rivers,
each carving its own course back to sea
to begin again the immortal water spiral,
so our species, like these rivers, rise
from the living rain of that great ocean, life,
and run and merge from manifold to fewer,
the trickles to the rivers, carving each
its own and special course of evolution,
to spill again into Life's vast ocean,
and begin again the immortal spiral, life.
Not from some old sire are we descended
but numberless drops of protoplasmic rain.

Here too at the start of our animal tale
we find a law recurs in it all through:
that every gain is paid for by some loss,
our animal freedom gained at the loss of roots
as later, lungs are gained at the loss of gills,
land by the loss of sea, feet for fins,
hands for feet, arms at the loss of wings,
the human brain for the brawn of dinosaur.
Is our forced freedom to suffer choice
of only an either-or, not both-and?
Can we choose both brains and brawn, hands and wings,
both land and sea, be amphibious once again,
and both at level higher pitched than ever?

Imagination runs too far ahead,
my Muse too keen to sing songs never sung:
she, the Muse of Nature, who too long
had lain like Beauty sleeping on her bed
till Science woke her from her too long dreaming.
His the labour: mine, truth's beauty singing.

(2)

Ocean, mother of us, bearer of all life,
alpha and omega, both the womb and tomb,
bearer of forms to startle wonder's eyes,
forms beautiful, gruesome, strange, or grim,
continuous miracles of living art
born of freedom upon necessity
as plopping pebble rings begets in a pool.

Blobs of live oil, jelly with soul inside,
deathless one-man cells our parents are
all us from them ascended. Mr Amoeba,
worthy sincere respect, a pioneer
of all our animal kingdom, common miracle
in which, of which, we have being, the wonder
in us, around us, above us, below us,
pervading us, before and after us –
the wonder even seeing hardly believes.

Grandpa Amoeba out of darkness coming
(Adam made by that all-chemist God)
in all his countless, infinite variety,
the simple cell, the unicellular soul,
self-sufficient hermit and cell in one
(cosmos of atoms, each a solar system)
nuclear, food-absorbing through all his mass
(all his hundredth part of an inch mass)
native to Nature's many kinds waters,
walking from waste on would-be feet away,
tentative explorer of world as yet unknown,
growing too big, divides himself by two
equally himself with himself sharing.
Comrade Amoeba, the first true socialist.

Amoeba is also our first true critic
discerning of taste, poison knowing from food,
discriminant of choice with his life at issue
though our poison at times his food may be,
for those amoebae our blood's white corpuscles
devour diseases that devour ourselves –

Doctor Amoeba, spendthrift in our defence.

Countless now as then and shall be ever
these first and last of anima-beings live
a life as everlasting as the sea
whose bed nevertheless their shells compose:
rootfeet, lash and lashes bearers, seeds
inhabit the guts of fleas, sheep, rats and men –
to microscopic eyes these creatures are
miracles of art and beauty, wonder profound
beyond imagination, beggaring genius,
profuse proliferation by the artist, Life.
What art can imitate the inimitable,
catch the Sun in a penny looking-glass
or sing the song of life, that greatest song,
but as boys may whistle airs Caruso sang?
Had I seen Bardot naked at her bath
what words could put such beauty down on paper?
Yet such task were unskilled labour's lot
compared to using mere words to convey
galaxic radiance of ray-animals,
the sun-animalcules, millions various forms
of filigreed tracery, delicate architecture,
intricate order perfect as paradise,
heaven-woven works of silica or limestone
at which wonder's thc first and last response:
and all souls, living, self-directing beings
that breathe, move, get, digest, excrete like us!
Some even have gardens in their fibres.

And all immortal, self-perpetuating,
living resurrections each and all!
Some of them, instead of would-be feet
their would-be roots put out (as if they looked
nostalgically back to the good old days
when they were plants still rooted in their Mother),
miraculous works of microscopic art:
others, tinier, wave their would-be whips
as though in compensation, the wee man's ego,
flogging the innocent water to get on:
some, sexual intercourse anticipate

and others multicellular colonies form;
some use hairs as men use oars or tillers
rowing about in garden ponds or oceans
or even in the water we drink; some
feed the mightiest animals on Earth;
others in termite intestines help digest wood;
some regenerate stock by sexual union;
others cause us many kinds diseases.

These everyday miracles everywhere around us
and even inside us, at large in gnats,
are facts fantastic beyond imagination,
far beyond even a Shakespeare's reach.

Think: of such wonders we are made,
and may indeed by some of them be unmade.

(3)

Safe from gravity down in the sea-bed world,
the realm at once of nightmare and of dream,
weightlessly building beautiful tenements,
endlessly variable sponges live in enclave,
a blind alley of animal evolution.
Single-celled souls but in colonies clustered
waving (some) their delicate fronds and fans
as if in breezes none of them normally know:
unimaginable forms, actually there,
of silica, lime or spongin fibres made.

What awesome maestro of Renaissance genius,
what Giotto, Leonardo, Buonarotti
created or could create the Carpenter's Glass,
Venus' Flower-basket (for young crustacea
a trap, as marriage for lovers) or the Glass-rope sponge –
perfection formally articulated?

Senseless, defenceless (having few enemies) sponges
simply waft water through their galleries,
food extracting and the waste expelling,
these tenement-dwellers in their niche of life
by no need forced to further evolve,
content in their own groove to live forever
while more ambitious species come and go:
tyrannosaurus, eryops, mastodon,
man himself, who knows? they will succeed
more millions years than even they preceded,
calmly static in their weightless world,
simple souls of colonised amoebae.
Yet if the lilies idling in their fields
outsplendoured Solomon's glorious array,
what of these glass-sponges outsplendour them?

Struggle for survival has passed them by:
or does survival prove that they're the fittest,
leaving lumbering behind the brachyosaurus,
megatherium, and their obsolete kind?
Gentle sponges, kindly refuge halls

for certain worms and other homeless creatures,
tolerant of such invading squatters,
aloof from the rat-race natural selection.

Yet they too produce their sperm and ova
freely floating, only by chance colliding,
the pregnant egg dividing like amoeba
till one becomes many, the many still one
new sponge that roots in the ocean bed.
There let life in their enclave leave them,
heirs of their under-water paradise.

(4)

The holy discontent Beethoven spoke of,
discontent with conditions as they are –
amoeboid forms, the individualist system –
made certain cells rebel against their lot,
get together in communistic bands,
dividing labour to serve their common needs
(special cells assigned their special tasks),
and took to the skin trade, hammering out in time
an outer pliable skin and an inner one,
with gluey stuff between, in a bell-like sack,
and the jellyfish was born. Made of the sea
itself they seem, repugnant-beautiful, leisurely,
gelatinously squeeze-propelled and hung
with tentacles, like oldtime ladies hats
or trailing streamers, each in fact a sting
charged with venom for defence and hunting.
Like the fabled serpent, they bring Death
into the world, death by division of labour
which deprives each specialising cell
of its immortality – the price paid
by complex organisms for their complexity.
Uncertain whether to range or stay at home,
whether to live like plants or animals,
they do both in alternate generations:
one in locomotion freely swimming,
the other plantlike on the sea-bed rooted,
the plant one sexless, yet its seed begetting
the sexual one. Imagine a human tribe
with mum and dad begetting higher apes,
those apes begetting humans in their turn!
Or imagine sedentary parents giving
birth to a generation of explorers,
they in turn to a generation of clerks:
or city tenement-dwellers alternating
with generations of restless, wandering tinks.

Manifold possibilities open up
with this two-skinned, division-of-labour system.
Many forms and species now can be

evolved by that superlative artist, Life,
and all within the laws that Nature sets
on all creation, animate or not –
the laws of mathematics, engineering,
architecture, physics and chemistry,
absolute truth, like two plus two make four
whether it be of spirochaetes or whales.
The other name of Truth, said Keats, is Beauty,
and Nature's truth indeed can be sublime
beyond the reach of art's loveliest fictions,
though not all truth is beautiful to us
for whom the Law of Predation is abhorrent,
and death and pain but relatively less so.
Nature is red indeed in tooth and claw,
taking the inhuman as her norm:
but though such horrors mar Life's greatest works,
the works themselves are no less marvellous.

Man-o-wars, aurelia, sea-firs,
coral polyps and sea-anemones,
sea-fans, sea-pens and other animal-flowers
and comb-bearers lovely as Venus' Girdle,
show the living Artist hard at work,
creating, testing, and experimenting,
saving, discarding, all to achieve – what?
Perfection in some earthly form of life?
Or is this living art for art's own sake?
Interrogate the winds on why they blow:
it's likely that the Artist does not know.
The Life-artist's earthly studio
is crammed with works of all hir many phases (hir: his-her)
periods, confraternity of works
from dashed-off scribbles to sublimest art –
for Life the Artist loves all equally,
each in its nature, equal but not the same,
with equal love, but not identical,
love of each in its own identity.
Identity's the primal law of species,
the law on which all other laws depend,
all form, tissue, structure, scale and growth:
all depend on identity of species
including their many metamorphoses.

(5)

This great conspiracy of Animation
having now achieved its brace of skins,
hangs poised upon invention of a third
(in embryo seen in some of these comb-bearers).
Now, like stout Cortez upon his Darien peak
(or young John Keats champing through Ilion corn)
comes the conquering lord of that frontier,
forging over its unbroken line – the flatworm,
the three skinned double-sider, no radial form
but head and tail, a right side and a left:
and where in jellyfish is medial jelly,
ripples in him the thew of the muscle-man
flexed for the tigrish spring upon his prey,
with nerves in system all but centralised,
ferocious of carnivorous appetite.

He it was on whom all hope depended
of ever venturing on that unknown, Land:
for this new form was able now to move
ranging and hunting over the ocean floor,
he the whirling worm, the worm of crowds,
turbulent hero of the wild frontier,
forging up the rivers and the streams
and even (some) onto Land itself,
the great barrier broken, to lurk under logs
fallen tree trunks, other woodland shelter:
surely the first invaders from the sea?
Cut him in six, you make him six new worms,
this cross-eyed little hero of evolution
shaped like a lime-leaf, bristling with equipment,
each with at least one penis, one vagina,
using both in coupling with hir fellows
each with penis in hir mate's vagina
fertilising and being fertilised
in weird hermaphroditic interchange
(did humans ever live a similar phase?)
yet they too by division multiplying.
Some fight battles with their penises!

No less in soul than body flatworm's gifted:
witness that green and convoluted one
goes up and down his sand-pit with the tide,
taking the Sun at the ebb, with the flow descending
like some old roué on the Riviera idling.
And all because ingeniously he solved
the whole animal problem since the fall
from being that self food-factory, a plant:
instead of eating plants to get their produce,
killing the goose that lays the golden eggs
and having to go on killing golden geese,
he simply takes in algae as his guests
to live in him, sharing what they produce,
as crofter-wives keep cattle for their milk.
How much might men, who murder golden species,
learn from that sapient, convoluted worm
twice daily taking, in Jersey, say, the Sun.

His cousin tube-worm also breaks new ground
by hammering out a circulation system
in his Nemertean lair among the rocks
where, creeping, he may grow to three score feet,
an elastic band that grows two selves if broken,
each complete with its digestive tract
(though eating and excreting through one hole),
circulation (though without a heart)
and fluid that is not unlike our blood.

The roundworm too a rousing triumph scores
by adding an anus to the digestive tract,
a kitchen and a shithouse in one tube.
Immense the vistas opened by these worms:
already the age of dinosaurs is near,
implicit in the tube-worms, wheelbearers,
the roundworms, and other of their kindred;
all distinctly either male or female.

Mighty as all their achievements are,
the ring-worms cap the lot — but not yet:
some other tribes between the two are set.

(6)

Crowned with tentacles, each its own king
among a colony of kings, each crown
a hungry maw by its own tentacles fed
like London by its provinces and outposts,
imperial centres fed by colonies,
the empires crowned together like departments
in a civil service or university –
such are the lace-corals and sea-mats,
complexities hidden in simplicities:
for not until the microscope reveals
the organised intelligence within
these mindless beings (mindless, yet made of mind
if only the artist Life's, the Mystery's)
can they be seen for the miracles they are.
Like sponges tenement-dwellers, and like corals
isolated together by common walls
uniting separate cells cemented apart:
a myriad Caesars bound apart together
in a myriad of microcosmic Romes.

(7)

Long before our race ever was, they were,
these beautiful but bound-by-tradition lamp-shells
that deep, though fathomed, caves of ocean bear,
double hands, like Dürer's clasped in prayer,
but rounder, smoother, more orthodox of form,
resistant to change, yet in life persistent
through (how many?) millions years anchored
to the sea-bed, death-defying living fossils,
living self-elegies, like Chinese script.

Like prairie Indians brinked upon extinction
in reservations herded for preservation
in living museums like zoological gardens,
half-worm, half-shellfish, wholly only themselves,
among our spineless souls by being themselves
they too serve, defying the categorist.

Like pearlless oysters in inaction rooted
they, with eyelash hairs, waft their victims
(they're beasts of prey) slowly along in waves,
as whales sift plankton, into their tentacled maws.
Armed with foot for hands, these creatures are
sexual in all but intercourse:
and some of those around our Hebrides
like sea-bed kangaroos, are marsupial –
How infinite of range, the Life artist,
how intricate of craft, like watch-makers
whose skills embrace the tiny and gigantic
in one all-in, engineering art.

Their future even longer than their past,
after our race has been will they still be?

(8)

Happy the soul that has a shell to hide in,
a door from which to keep the world's wolf:
no naked worm to all life's dangers open!
Would not old Lear, unkempt on the storm-clawed moor,
have given his kingdom, damned daughters and all,
for a man-sized shell to clam into that night?
Happy the shellfish then in mortgaged homes
that revert to Death, the owner, in the end,
to furnish a while some feckless hermit home
and shelter from a cold, inhuman world,
seeming security and a social stake,
a pauper hostel hidden from the light.
But no, I let our human world break in
too brutally on Nature's innocence,
on buckies, limpets, periwinkles, whelks,
clams, mussels, oysters, cowries, snails,
their jazzy shells from Nature's sweetie shop
baked for children by the Confectioner,
whirls and whorls, bulges, spirals, fringes,
scallops and fretted edges, and all colours,
spotted, striped and barred, draperies fluted,
tucked, rucked, multiform of design
as if by an aesthete Nature only made
to delight the sense in a world of sense-delight,
all creatures made to please each other's eyes.

Simple coat-o-mail shell, stomach-pipes
old as earliest fossils in the rocks,
lightly they wear their hundreds millions years,
bypassing Darwin and that jungle rat-race,
long outliving a thousand fittest survivors,
ungoaded by the need for Getting On:
but if no winners, no losers either,
content to rest with their appointed lot
as any tortoise ever outran a hare,
any Wheel-freed Buddha under his bo-tree.

Consider the humble clam, how far it's come
from amoeba or the primal protoplasm:

squelchy body clamped in iron shells,
enclosed in its immobile skeleton.
Near all man's organs in that squelch you'll find
between those shells: a foot with sinuses,
muscles, ligaments, joint-hinges, blood,
stomach, intestines, mouth and anus, glands,
membranes (mucus and other), lips, throat,
ventricles, auricles in aortaed heart,
no brain but ganglia of nerves, veins,
liver, kidneys, gonad, ovaries, testes
as well as organs humans haven't got –
various tubes and siphons, gills, plates,
ostia, umbo, concentric growth lines, mantle,
a nacreous layer as well as a prismatic,
a periostracum, a pallial line,
and a brood-chamber not unlike the womb –
all that in the tiniest of clams,
and much the same in cockles, mussels, oysters
(pearl-creating, not-so simple souls
preyed upon by starfish, whelk, and man).
A long way to come on a single foot,
no map, and by trial and error method,
no schooling but the schooling of the sea,
no help but the life-urge, and the Mystery.

With all that, how could Land resist?
Out of the sea there came the intrepid snail
the rover, viking, at first on daring raids
but gradually settling on the land
making there hir home and slimy roads,
taking over, making the land hir own,
a pack-backed prospector, staking hir claims
far from the haunt and realm of hir cousin clams.
But for hir this song could not be sung,
no nor greater far than this can be,
the songs of Homer, Dante, Shakespeare, Goethe:
nor giant such as Bach, Mozart, Beethoven
ever could have reached the gates of heaven
to let men catch a glimpse of paradise:
the Sistine Chapel roof had never known
the godlike touch of Michelangelo,

the stone concerto of San Pietro's dome
had never raised a soul to the sublime,
there to receive the deathless kiss of God.

Therefore it becomes men to recall,
in every such moment of privilege,
the monumental debt they owe to snails
and other of our animal forefathers,
God's children also, for their labour.
Don't cynically think that I descend
to mere bathos, linking the snail and God:
the Nazarene was cradled in a byre.

Snail, I say – but was it not some limpet
geared to withstand two thousand times its weight
exerted by the ravenous brute waves,
a rock on which to build the church of Man?
More likely some amphibian river snail,
the kind that can, armed with both gill and lung,
from marsupial pouch produce its young alive,
a crosser of rubicons, from sea to land,
from amphisex to differentiation,
gills to lungs, hermaphroditic Caesar
by decisive action crossing over
to seize power on his own authority
or that of the life-urge (say that I AM hath sent you).
Was this the hero of that old Greek tale
how amphisex was parted into boy
and girl, both fated forever after
to wander lovelorn through this lonely world,
each seeking other with agonised devotion?
Narcissus and his sister love-divided?
Orpheus and Eurydice in hell?
Eros and Psyche yearning for each other?

The search has taken these two star-crossed lovers
all over Earth, from marram-edged sea-beaches
far up the Andes and sky-cloaked Himalayas,
from girdled equator to polar circles:
and where their trail they blazed, we men have followed,
followed in the footsteps of a snail.

But most of these squelch-bodies are not made
of such heroic mettle, but remain
down in the weightless fathoms of the sea,
in their evolutionary rut content to stay
change-abhorring, clammy conservatives
ambitious to be left ambitionless,
untoiling serfs in mindless sea-bed bondage
rooted in their plate-gilled double shells
passively fed by every nursing tide,
bloomless lilies. Yet some such mother pearls
sit in crowns that sit on kings and queens,
and long outlive such royal ephemera.

(9)

The horn old wreathed Wordsworth's Triton blew
was almost certainly cast by yon argonaut
the pearly nautilus, many-chambered sailor –
unless he'd stored some shells of ammonite
from palaeolithic or Devonian times.

Those wavy curves, crescendoing convolutions
(like some extinct wee elephant's cut-off trunk
curled in on itself), could tell such tales
if they were tongued, of aeons before man
was even possible to evolution:
tales, rooted in the primeval swamps,
of creatures never can to us be known
yet common when the nautilus was young,
as well as those known only fossily to us
(straighthorns, ammonites and curledhorns)
by the irrefutable witness of the rocks,
all four-gilled creatures, far already advanced
on evolution's coiling, curling climb –
those octopuses brooding in their shells.

And like a nautilus turned inside out
the octopus we know today began,
all devouring arms and knowing head
and sleepless eyes that never miss an alga,
quick on the trigger of responsive nerves,
inventor and master of defensive smoke-screen
(unused by men before their first world war)
master, too, of camouflage and evasion,
a shy monster parrot-beaked for prey,
quick to learn though lacking a proper brain,
slippery as any politician,
slithering over rocks as he over facts.

No such slithering marks the whizz-kid squid
jet-propelled, stream-lined and arrow-headed
submarine rocket, lightning as any flasher
when need compels him to a burst of speed.
Like the octopus ever-open of eye,

this ancient scribe armed with pen and ink
to his eight arms adds two tentacles –
the biggest spineless beast on land or sea.
Strange he has never tried to conquer land:
though three-hearted, pluri-brained, he lacks
the courage and resource of snails and worms
to press on bravely into that unknown,
though sometimes he may equal, length for length,
the sperm whales whose mighty prey he is.
Titanic the convulsions must at times
torture the depths and surface of the sea
(as Bullen once in moonlight chanced to witness)
giant squid and whale in battle locked,
mighty jaws embraced by strangling arms
(lucky for the whale he has no neck),
the suckers tearing skin from blubbery flesh,
the great jaws mangling rather than biting off
thirty-foot long tentacles and arms
in threshing blood-and-sepia turbulence –
a sight to make the games of Rome look tame.

Romance among these beasts is rather classical,
(though crowding the whitened seas like festival ghosts)
practical common-sense devoid of passion.
Romeo simply hands his Juliet
a gift-box of his capsulated sperm
to impregnate her ova with – and she
then plants her fertilised eggs in the ocean bed.

Practical too is yon paper nautilus
perambulates her young through pearlous seas
in a beautiful and fluted nacre pram.

(10)

What kind of kingdom is it has no king,
no single brain to centralize, control
the criss-cross network of our nervous system?
Our animal society lacked a head
till forward strode a mighty pioneer,
a Charlemagne from a heroic clan
to crown himself king, meeting the people's need.
With body built like beads to required length,
with nervecentres in its every segment
but all controlled by an overseeing brain,
the ringed worm takes evolution's stage.
So the ragworm, like returned Ulysses
hides beneath his rags a kingly power
of organisation subtle and complex.
Take Nereis, the offspring of a sea-god,
wife devouring, sex-changing (some),
astonisher of the orthodox and dull,
a masterpiece of living evolution
lost among the wonders of the ocean,
four-eye-headed, fiercely tentacled, jawed,
each segment splaying a foot each side
like matching oars on some oddly even scull,
an anatomy makes the clam seem primitive,
a blood system already much like man's
closed in vessels, full of haemoglobin,
a sprung tiger to pounce on prey
and drag it down into his tearing den:
on summer nights clouding the sea with spawn
responsive to some calling by the Moon,
that pallid mistress of her devoted ocean,
all-controller of its times and seasons.

So the creeping sea-mouse, Aphrodite
(in honour of the erotic goddess named
because she's like a beautiful, silky quim)
beneath her iridescent fur-coat
secretes the complex body of a worm;
and scores of others of such magical kind,
many like flowers, or flowers in a vase,

others like eccentric millipedes.

So, too, that humble friend of men
entitled as the Worm of Mother Earth,
that faithful peasant, tiller of the soil
whom Burns inexplicably forgot
to celebrate among his fellow-mortals,
the ploughman's friend and topsoil over-turner
(ten tons per year per acre, Darwin says,
of soil swallowed and as casts excreted),
mankind's, indeed all earthkind's benefactor:
creatures, too, of taste, sensitive
even, it is said (though blind) to light.
O wriggler tortured on the hooks of boyhood,
no wonder I soon turned to feathered fly,
shrinking from the horrors of my sport
(but still am Esau, still at heart the hunter)
to such effect that ever since, I've tried
in recompense to rescue stranded worms
flushed by rain out onto city pavements.

So even those sucking parasites
attack the starfish, urchins and sea-lilies;
even Dr. Leech, that arrant quack
whose toll of lives makes Hornbook's look paltry,
who did for Byron (that repulsive bard
whose treatment of his daughter earned no less,
though with the goose we lost some golden eggs).
Leeches that in Amazonian forests,
tropical jungles, bush and mangrove swamp,
spring like beasts of prey on travellers –
they too are heroes in our animal fable:
they too are major branches of the Tree.

(11)

The fool hath said in his heart there is no God,
yet even a fool can see God everywhere
manifest throughout the universe
in every living miracle of being.
God's all that is, and all that is is God
(that early Teuton term for 'Reality')
though not of course yon puerile nobodaddy,
Santa Claus with gifts and a hangman's rope,
the Roman executioner's mell and nails,
the Jewish murderer of scapegoat sons
offering Isaacs up on the ego's altar:
nor other blasphemies of the living God.

No. Let me show God to you where
the first rays of the Sun are glinting on
the dew-white filaments by a spider woven
there in the twigs of yon old hawthorn hedge,
octagonal cathedral of the life
that preys on life, as all life preys
by God's own will, on God (this bread ... this blood ...)

Let me show you God not only in
the configured night's cold amaze of stars
and all that vast astonishment of space
but also where the golden cow-fly feasts
there on that steaming dung, where the innocent ewe
with cold and mindless eye bunch-munches clover,
where hovers the dragon-fly in the rustling sedge
and Jenny Longlegs helicopters down
toward that kingfisher broods upon the pool
where the water-boatman rows with sturdy stroke.

God is everything and everywhere,
everywhen, and beyond thing, where and when,
beyond he, she, or it or us or them.
God is the icicle edging the winter weir,
the purl of the burn in spring or any season,
the humble Water of Leith forever flowing
down from Harperrig, down past Balerno,

Currie, down through Colinton Dell to Slateford,
Murrayfield, Dean Village and Stockaree,
patiently bearing insult and abuse,
polluted with garbage, tin-cans, bicycle wheels,
past Bonnington and on to Leith itself,
there to blossom out in languid swans,
to endure the harbour's oiled indignity
and find rest in the bosom of the Firth:
flowing now as it was flowing then
a million years before there (yesterday) was
ever an Arthur breeked to name a Seat –
and will flow on a million years from now.

God's all that is, nought is that is not God.
No evil is, save in the human will
and even there is not because of sin
but because our light with dark is clouded over.

Nature and God are aspects of each other;
one universe, their bible, holy writ
made manifest in things, sermons indeed
in stones, rock-strata, books in the running burns,
the master-text of everything that is
wherein all those who can acquire the key
may read the inner workings of God's mind
and the processes of that arch-artist, Life.
All a revelation that only leads
to deeper depths of Mystery behind,
and greater wonder at the living God.
The only book that Dante could not read
but the only one God makes compulsory.
Theology Dante deemed queen of sciences:
for us Science is of theologies queen,
revelations of Reality,
for God we know only as we know the wind
that worries our hair, races over the corn
as over waves of ocean, harasses trees
and sets their leaves whirling and scurrying,
tears up townships in its tornado mood
and devastates whole lands and continents –
yet no man has ever seen a wind

not taken its height, depth and thickness:
so the invisible God, our own Creator
is known to us only as mysterious force
both hidden and revealed in all creation,
planets and stars, genera and species,
deducible only as being by manifest doing:
the stooping falcon is God in action,
and God looks out through every eye there is.

(12)

Quest for a skeleton begins with shells,
hard structures to protect the flesh,
the living organism, from hostile forces;
inorganic matter defending organic
thus conscripted, made by division of labour.
But just as the medieval fortress
also was the jailer of free movement,
so to snail and clam and even tortoise
defensive armour has its handicaps.
But what if shell be made to help not hinder
movement, just as mobile machines do Man?
Suppose you turn the shell inside the flesh
or keep the flesh inside the armoured shell,
but make of it articulate machines
designed to do the work you have to do?
The inturned shell becomes a skeleton
may lead to that of the vertebrates and Man:
the outturned one becomes a chiton case
as used by beetles, lobsters, bees and ants,
the medieval fortress now discarded
for mobile armies, tanks and armoured cars.

The inorganic, hard machinery
makes possible increased mobility
far in advance, for power and quality,
of anything the jellyfish could do,
the squid, the worm, or other spineless things:
just as a central core of hard fact
made of Barbour's BRUS 'a suthfast tale'
and makes a structured poetry of this Tree
will longer than pure poesy stand to time.

Starfish lead the way that leads to man,
hedgehog-fingered fists to prise a clam
or oyster, hard and horny hands that walk
the rocks and hazards of the sea-bed world,
sea-urchin, brittle-star and sea-cucumber,
some like knights in armour mailed in limestone,
others delicate fronds like the sea-lilies;
but they too are imprisoned by their choice.

The mail outlives the flesh, as gold outlives
those who sell their souls for sake of it.
Like Portia suitors, each gets what he chooses
for all time: like Paolo and Francesca
married in a fuck no orgasm ends.
So each chooses and bears his consequence,
fur or scale or feather, fin or wing
or hand or hoof — or even hedgehog skin
like these pentangle starfish, by whose sign
Gawain rode out to meet the Grene Knight,
that perfect nature dressed in Nature's hue.
But they've no head, these ocean stars, to lose,
these independent hands, grasps incarnate,
stomachs everting into ravished clams.

Yet Nature favours most the vulnerable,
not the ironclads, the dinosaurs:
favours most of all the accessible girl.
And if Christ comes again, it is as woman,
vessel of the future of the species.

All these frangible snaketails, tangled strings
of Christmas tinsel, straggly madonnas, seem
at times a growing-place for cleverer forms
than mailed fists with stomachs as their palms,
than non-explosive mines on the sea-bed trundling,
heroes of evolution begetting greater.
Seem? Take these things as they are, sun-stars
giving our Lord sincerest flattery;
urchins leaving tests the Druids called
sea-serpents' eggs, sacred to the Goddess;
writhing gorgon-heads no neck upholds;
sea-cucumber with the curious habit
not only of breathing through its anus
but of keeping a pet fish in it as well!
Chinese trepang, these bêches-de-mer for a soup
(furnishing like Jesus forth a supper)
yet able to protect themselves from lobster,
slugs though they seem, exuding poisonous slime
and, as politicians can their principles,
discarding guts and growing themselves new ones.

See too those animals on stalks
the cup-shaped sea-lilies, flower-headed
multitudinous life in frightening profusion
coming from times before we ever were
or ever could have been, we upstart humans,
youngest child of the Earth that we despoil,
who forewent Adam longer than Adam me,
those simple souls our Rosy Feather-stars
on falling plankton feeding, on a drizzle of death.

(13)

Halfway between a ringedworm and a jointleg
peripatus comes, the walker-abouter,
worm with claw feet and jointless legs
but looking like some squelchy caterpillar,
troubler of classifiers' tidy minds,
ruggedly himself, this plodding misfit
dodges the pigeon-holer, the label-sticker,
the mud-slinger, the evil slanderer
who smears the very saints with his vile labels
and would leave even a Blake without good fame –
though peripatus holds his own at smearing,
whether for defence or taking prey.
Segmented like the worm, like insect breathing,
many-footed as a centipede,
peripatus brings forth young alive
like any mammal, but leaves them feed themselves:
another beast no off-the-peg suit fits.

(14)

To conquer land in all its millions miles
true legs are needed, sturdy jointed limbs
to stride forth like ambulating cranes
firm to support, able to master acres.
Enter such conquistadores now,
legs of crab and lobster to scuttle over
the floors of not so silent seas, legs
of crayfish, prawn and shrimp, of water-fleas;
but also legs of centipede and beetle,
cockroach, earwig, cricket, bug and fly,
legs of ant and termite, spider legs.
Armies of colonisers for the land
turning their backs forever on the sea,
or a last look at the grey waves rolling in,
seeing the swelling ridge riding ashore,
dull glassy surface rippling here and there
in fleeting mobile ribs and slopes and ledges,
creasing and spraying as its piling volume
dimples and swirls from underneath the surface,
with little spirts and jets and spurts breaking
the highest crests of the long ridge rolling
building up on nearing, while offspring wavelets
streak off waywardly across the slope
of ragged, trembling wall, till it uprears
and crashes forward, frothy-white in its fall,
myriad-splinter splashing in bubbling surge
of creamy foam, countless fairy gaspings,
diving headlong as if it had been tripped up
by the backrush of the get-away wave in front,
the whole swashling ashore, hissing and gurgling,
wide-spread foaming in one long frothy run
that levels out in purling, bursting bubbles –
then falls back under the next one, back to sea.

More numerous far than the other animals totalled
(seven hundred and fifty thousand species)
these joint-legs rival in many ways mankind,
some surpassing all but the human primates
(surpassing even them in many ways),

dispute with man his consulship of Earth
and may, who knows, when that destructive species
(born as much of Satan as of God)
Nature indignantly hustles from the scene,
succeed him as a far superior form
(Kafka's beetle a vision of Messiah?)
that saves the Earth from man's improvidence.

Kin of the trilobites of the ancient rocks
come all such creatures, comes their gorgeous
flower show of butterflies and moths
which I'll not try to fix with pinning words,
'Psyche' in Greek, both butterfly and soul,
honoured to be loved by the god of love himself,
Eros, son of deathless Aphrodite:
image of the love of gods and humans.

The sense of wonder living things inspire
auxiliary feelings may attend,
love, compassion, fear, distaste, repulsion,
and of this leggy clan I know are some
one finds it very hard indeed to love,
these suits of armour with no knight inside.
Could you caress a live tarantula?
Could even St. Francis love his scorpion brother?
All Eve's Miss Muffet at sight of the mildest spider.
And if there is a heaven, does it crawl
with souls of centipedes and millipedes,
earwigs, ants, stag and rhinoceros beetles,
ichneumons, longhorns, bugs and praying mantis,
fleas and lice and those mighty creatures, mites?
Does its air hum to the tune of Monsieur Mosquito,
drone with the buzz of hornet, wasp and bee:
flutter with fritillary and red admiral,
with emperor and malagasy moth,
peacock-eye and birthwort butterflies?
And are the spectral woods of paradise
bored by the giant woodwasp, saw-flies, horntails?
I do not know, but if there is a heaven,
be sure that God runs no Men Only club,
no bunny-girl haven for playboy souls

with gonococcus barred, the spirochaete.

Easier count the countless stars in space
than enumerate these many-jointed creatures
much less nominate this commonest clan
(eight million insects pinned in the British Museum)
and I for one have no desire to try.
But some there are stand out among the rest
as greater wonders do among the lesser:
dityscus with his bubble under his arm,
mortally afraid of his own son;
Mrs horseshoe crab at her tail dragging
six or seven husbands up the beach
to her breeding-place, outwiving the Wife of Bath;
the fairy tadpole in her arctic puddle
active six weeks of summer, her eggs frozen
forty weeks or so in arctic ice
yet can survive heat at boiling-point
as well as cold three-sixty under zero;
Salt Lake City, tabernacle-choired,
whose eyes have seen the glory of the coming
of the Lord and flights of angel seagulls
sweeping down on the ruinous locust plague
(a plague of awesome miracles themselves),
yet little heeds, deep in the Great Salt Lake
the little brine shrimp, odalisque in red,
swimming on her back with languid feet
not beckoning her lover but wafting food
gently mouthward, virgin mother of eggs
can lie in dry mud dormant many years
then spring to life as did the Sleeping Beauty
as soon as touched by the charming kiss of rain.

In the image of what God's the water-flea made,
that self-important provost, that burgher-bellied
little fuss-pot waving his praising hands?
Did he who made Man make the barnacle
nauplius (six-legged, one-eyed, one-shelled)
becoming cypris (twelve-legged, two-eyed, two-shelled)
becoming barnacle (eyeless and feather-legged)?
Or that seventeen-year locust lives but days

then dies, having laid eggs hatch out in six weeks
larvae that sleep in the ground for seventeen years
then rise as locusts, lay eggs, live but days?

The living God has images in millions
(twelve hundred thousand of them animal species)
and is beyond all such imaginings;
has spider ideas, termite forms in mind,
prawn thoughts and crab and lobster moods
O endlessly playful, practical-joking Deity!
Imagine a coconut crab, ancient bushman's
eight gnarled fingers loose in an old maid's bed!
The joke at times is carried to extremes,
as round Japan the giant spider crab
whose spindleshanks on the floor of Honshu seas
may span three yards or more without breaking.
One thing of the God of Life seems true:
whatever can be done, Life will do it,
defining limits by exceeding them
in height, in depth, in length, breadth and thickness;
energy in identity in environs
in time, governs all form and growth,
and Identity is the fundamental law:
a rose is a rose and persists to be a rose,
for interbreeding's taboo between the species.

Yet endlessly experimenting, never
confusing media, Life the divine Artist,
faithful to the nature of each kind,
explores all possibilities in time
demonstrating deftly infinite dexterity
bound by necessity (as poems by their matter)
far beyond what the human mind can follow,
for the Mystery increases with our knowledge.
Why, is the question Science cannot answer.

(15)

What God does hermit crab look like in its shell
anemone-capped, bristle-worm inside?
Or yon light that you may see in Epping Forest
walking in the dark on a hundred legs
as love lights a courting centipede's way:

> Centipede, centipede burning bright
> In Epping Forest of a night,
> What immortal erotessence
> Furnished you with phosphorescence?

And tell me what slave-driving God of toil
are ants and bees made in the image of?
They who yet may supersede mankind
as proletarians the bourgeoisie?
Busy, discriminant ant, finely fastidious,
fussily feeling over possible foodstuffs,
carnivegivorous all-grist maw-mills,
enslaved slavers, some with fungus gardens,
granaries of somehow sterilised seeds,
worshippers of an immobile long-lived queen
(Rider Haggard's model for his She?),
more strictly caste then can be any humans,
soldiers put out fires with their own bodies
(thus outspartaning Thermopylae)
damming streams in the selfsame manner
(as Russian dead blocked roads at Stalingrad) –
terrors who empty jungles of their fauna.
Their anthill one beast made of a million beasts,
communism without a human face,
puritanism without a trace of beauty,
finally ugly as their bloated queen.
But one thing they've with Solomon in common:
they too by the idle lilies are outgloried.

Yet queen of all this vast and leggy clan
(outnumbering all others put together)
is one of mankind's cattle – the honey-bee
miller of food for bees, men, saints and gods,
modestly dressed in brown, and thankless toil.

Zip! Four o'clock of a summer day,
a new queen goes soaring up at the Sun
and on her tail, like a charge of outsize buckshot,
a hundred ardent drones in their one moment,
each of them with fifty thousand eyes,
these petted dandies of the hive, for this
moment of high ecstacy prepared.
In that one hectic dazzling aspiration
every serial acrobatic trick
she tries in dodging her pursuing lovers:
but one air-ace, outdistancing the others,
homes in on her back like kamakaze,
strikes, and in that wild career they crash,
pause, and fall precipitately down,
he in ecstatic death having shot his load
to be torn by her in pieces on the ground,
his single load of sperm enough for her
to fertilize a thousand eggs a day with
all the five or six years of her life
(as many years as worker-bees live weeks),
not counting drones she makes of unspermed eggs.

And the other drones, the unsuccessful ones?
The very bees that petted them for the flight
starve them on their return, beat them senseless
and sweep them out of the hive to lingering death,
so many Belisariuses degraded.

One bee in fifty thousand made a queen
can keep that fifty thousand from declining
although her subjects' paltry six-week lives
are ending by a thousand every day:
poor, sterile worker-girls, mere slaves
worn out by feeding pollen-mush and honey
to the queen's thousand babies daily born.
She lives, in human terms, four thousand years.

Bees with their bee language dance and touch
to learn from their scouts exactly what direction
and distance what exactly flowers are found,
how many exactly workers it needs to frisk them

and exactly how much fuel they need for the trip,
their go and return timed by internal clock,
supping nectar made by the flowers for bees
and bees alone, using and being used:
they're the precision engineers of the clan,
the practical intellectuals, rivalling man.

You think that only man has intellect,
only man has engineering skill?
No, man alone imagination possesses
but many creatures have brilliant intellects.
Other creatures build their own skyscrapers:
man alone can write poems and plays.

(16)

With systems of digestion, circulation,
respiration, excretion, reproduction,
of growth and form and nervous distribution,
sensory and metasensory lines
of communication, with skins, glands and muscles,
weapons of predation, defence and attack,
locomotion by air, sea and land,
these vast Tartarean hordes of joint-legged folk
have travelled far indeed from their beginnings
in those simple souls the one-celled animals.
What worlds are left to conquer?
Sea-squirts
(humbler far than spider, ant or bee)
vegetating there on the ocean-bed
nevertheless when young hint at a spine,
soon lost as they grow down to adulthood
(as young apes rival humans for a time).
With that true knight Sir Lancelet Amphioxus
the spinal cord begins, though like Gawain's
green opponent, doing without a head.
And in that hungry latcher the twisting lamprey
a spine and brain are quite discernible:
and in his pioneering wake sweep in
shark and ray and nightmare rabbitfish.
The spinal cord and brain take over ocean.

(17)

Sharks, by man cast in criminal roles,
the spivs and gangsters of ocean underworld,
anti-social psychos, tearaways,
are really no such things, they're only sharks;
torpedoes incarnate, of leisurely grace and beauty,
of coarse steel, yet somehow weak and chinless,
these easy masters of their water medium
old as the rocks, or seeming nearly so,
almost of fish the aboriginal stock.

Cousteau and Hass, Kon-tiki Heyerdahl,
bold ambassadors of ours to Neptune,
less intimidating facts report.
They have the self-assurance of the strong
rather than the malice of the weak
(who has not seen a coiffured poodle yap
at some tail-wagging, mildly surprised Great Dane?).
So it seems that sharks invading men
(whether armed with cameras or spears)
eye with curiosity or respect
unless the scent of blood should trigger off
the food-complex, as lust in men by perfume,
turning them into tigers of the sea.
Even the great whale shark, that sixty-footer,
seems no more a menace than the whale
or dolphin who in play cavorts with man
(Hass in the Red Sea rode one bareback)
while basking sharks of course like baleen whales
live only on the smallest of sea creatures,
only by accident bumping into boats
with all their languid tons of torpid flesh.

Blue sharks, mysterious hammer-heads
with eyes upon peninsulas outposted,
swift and avid foragers of ocean,
know no lust (like man's) for cruelty –
though much of animal life to us seems cruel,
there is no cruel animal but man.
No carpet, no bull-headed shark, no spur-dog

ever wielded the tawse, the birch, the cat,
the knout, the red-hot pincers, the rack, the wheel,
the bastinado, electric or water torture,
hangman's rope, the stake, the pale, the cross,
nor ever indulged in tortures of the mind
from the science of psychology derived –
deprivation of sound, Solitary,
unconscious tortures of psychiatric wards –
nor vivisected their fellow animals,
nor forced poor dogs to chain-smoke till they die,
nor other of men's myriad deviltries.
Imagination man alone possesses.

These primitives, the specialists assure us,
in some respects are nearer us than fish are,
copulating and bearing young alive
instead of tossing spawn about the ocean
or on the beds of stifling burns like salmon:
and some of them are civilization's food –
the monk or angel-fish (though miscalled Dory
or sold in little bits as pseudo-scampi),
and London's own 'rock salmon' is a dogfish:
both of them but smaller kinds of shark.

And those poor tramped-on sharks, the flattening rays
hugging the sand they have been ground into
under the weight of ocean's heel, prostrate
as some steam-rollered Disney-cartoon beast
(except for those great spectres flapping through ocean,
the manta rays the Hasses gambolled with,
their shovellers wafting strombs at their wide mouths)
are surely the most primitive of all;
some with whips, some armed with poison-stings
or with electric charge can stun a horse,
weird as rabbitfish, chimaeras, those
distortion-mirror caricatures of fish,
Darwinian nightmares by Life incarnated,
products of some oceanic slum.

Life with these creatures has advanced a pace,
has mobile jaw, a spine, a skull, a brain,

has sprouted limbs (two fore-fins, two hind –),
and new ventures by air and land now open.
But cartilage is too pliant to run on,
or to hold a beast aloft upon the wind:
as bronze to iron in later times give way,
cartilage must now give way to bone.

(18)

Great star! author of all our being,
of Earth itself, and every earthly thing
whether quick with soul or not alive,
pivot and source of all your circling nine,
O Sun, divine light and heat on whom
we all depend for every breath of being,
each least cell, receive a son's praise,
a prodigal's return from man-made gods
to your true light in that cosmic Mystery
surrounding even you as dark a candle.

Lighten our darkness, warm our cold hearts
to microcosmic suns in our own circles,
kindle in us, can you?, love of our kin,
our animal kindred, each one in its kind,
all Earth's children, our fellow-mortals
and poor earth-born companions. Help us deserve
our unbought, unearned, heritage of Earth,
sharing freely what is freely given,
not charging others for what you give to all,
the benefits all life gets free from you.
For humans rob each other of your gifts
setting up robber laws against that Law
governs even you and cosmic Nature,
a thief society (over your community)
founded upon division born of the fruit
of the tree of illusion of knowledge of good and evil
(knowledge no more given to mere men
than is the fruit of the Tree of Life itself),
setting humans above reality.

Turn our hearts away from coveting
the moon or other planets than our own,
to work for peace, to make our Earth a place
all other planets might think paradise,
one vast nature park, mankind the warden
in harmony living with our animal kin:
the nightmare Profit and her monstrous brood
extinct as the cretaceous dinosaurs,

the capitalist monsters out of place
in the Human Age as they in the Age of Mammals.
Turn our hearts indeed to peace on Earth
as Ikhnaton, your son, too early tried to
(by priests of darkness, prisoned in their time,
would-be exiled in the eternal wastes)
but resurrected in the Prince of Peace
and living now and forever in your rays
beyond the power of any priest-usurper
standing between the peoples and the light,
lackeys of any rascal comes to reign –
Caesar, king, or mere prime minister.

From all false creeds and dogma spawned by men
(but claiming your authority and name)
deliver us, all such abominations,
idols made by priests to snare our souls
and crucify the ever-living God
with monstrous tales of sin and punishment
that outrage Nature, goodness, truth and beauty,
hoisting Evil on high and calling it Good,
teaching worship of Death in the name of Life
Everlasting, blighting the lives of generations
with wicked calumnies of the God of Life,
scarring history with such shameful wounds –
heathen and jew, christian, pagan, moslem,
the cross, the sword, the faggot and the stone.
What Faith has not prepared the torture chamber?
Blasphemed God as a God of genocide?
The history of 'faith' is scarred with horror
Jerusalem, Jericho, Carthage and Provence,
Atahualpa, Wishart, Polynesia
where priceless cultures died in the name of Christ,
Belsen and Treblinka – blasphemy!

Our Father which art indeed in heaven
or in, at any rate, 'the heavens' as we say
make clean our hearts with your redemptive rays,
make whole our sick societies and race,
O Star among a shore of stars, O Sun
cathedralled in your corner of the Cosmos,

your congregation everything that lives,
your God the cosmic Mystery (to man)
whose reflection you are (as we are, or should be, yours)
help us to find health again in you.

The contradictions wrecking civilization
expose — Profit's deadly war on wages;
Usury's making money out of nothing;
financiers stealing (as 'money') social credit;
Governments forging notes that no goods back,
mortgaging nations by this secret tax;
Banking's evil trade in currencies
abusing notes of credit as market goods
as ticket-touts inflate the worth of tickets.
Expose the factors menace earthly life
subverting Nature and her evolution —
industrial wastes that poison land and sea,
the foods we eat, the very air we breathe,
men's improvident ravaging of Earth
threatens whole species and Man himself with murder
by atomic fall-out, microbes, man-made monsters,
oil and fumes pollution, man-made hell
ruled by the devil Car and all his fiends,
idolaters who worship him as God,
living corpses coffined in machines.

Let your light play on hidden, unhealthy things,
on civil servants usurping the people's rule,
financial cabals, cartels and cornerings,
monopolies, the banks, the stock exchanges,
Mafias and all freemasonries
whether of race, religion, party, creed,
and that most damned conspiracy of all,
Society rigged against Nature and her peoples,
feeding the face that fits, depriving the others
of all God's indiscriminate gifts to all,
sin against the community of Life,
that true unit of further evolution.
Reveal the dead bones under the papal robes,
the enemy of Life beneath the mitre,
the superstitious witch-hunter beneath

the sage brow of the state psychiatrist,
his nose sharp for political heresy;
the power-lust disguised as 'authority',
the face of Satan leering down from the cross.

Show us the lies in the politician's 'truth',
illuminate our slums of town and mind,
heal with your rays the rickets of the soul,
lay bare each communal sore, each festering wound
of man's inhumanity to man and beast
that makes O untellable millions mourn.
Restore the countries die at a tyrant's whim,
financier's word or politician's dictat,
expose the criminal under the judge's wig,
victims of contempt of contemptible courts,
Injustice coiled upon the throne of Justice
(Evans, Hanratty, Meehan and many others),
senile delinquents self-righteously raving
at juvenile ones they far surpass in crime,
the greatest crimes committed by 'the law'.

Visit on all our sufferings and defeats
the benison of your medicinal rays,
make all our East Ends Edens of the soul –
not mine, not his, not hers, but our communal soul,
salvation not of the person but the species.
Let commerce wither, the childishness of markets.
Let the maturity of mankind begin,
heal our hurt hearts – O make us well!

(19)

Who's poet enough to sing the song of bone?
Not that I mean the 'bone beneath the skin'
that Webster with his death-obsession sang
and Lovell Beddoes in more recent times:
I mean what civilization's founded on,
the marvellous articulated bone
made Memphis possible, Nineveh, Babylon,
created (music in stone) the Parthenon,
grasped Virgil's, Dante's, Shakespeare's, Goethe's pen;
those fingers brought to life the Last Supper,
ceilinged Capella Sistina with paradise,
held the tools that worked Ghiberti's gates
and sculpted the David, Moses and Pieta;
that handled Bach's great organ, Mozart's keyboard;
Beethoven's fist that knocked on the gates of heaven;
the fingers raced across Chopin's piano;
the hands that built the great wall of China,
the Taj Mahal, San Pietro, Santa Sophia
and other marvels I have only heard of –
Great God! who isn't poet enough
to sing the praise of such a benefactor!

Therefore think of what it is we owe
to the humble bichirs of the Nile, the sturgeon,
spoonbills, the reedfish of West Africa
and other early pioneers of bone,
some of them foreshadowing the lung
as they broke the water-surface to gulp air.
The sturgeon's worth's not weighed in caviare
nor in isinglass the worth of its air-bladder.
Fast now disappearing from the world
the bowfin and Cyrano-snouted gar-pike
(though to none but starving strays a food),
have given a thrust to their branch of our Tree –
on evolution's frontiers done good service,
too soon joining the died-out herring-mouths
who pioneered all equal vertebrae
and sired our herrings, wide-mouths, trout and salmon:
some of the noblest fish in any water.

A hundred pounds of tarpon, armed in plated
silver, leaps at the sun from spurned waves,
writhes a glinting missile in the air
and crashes back into the outraged ocean.
Hir cousins, the sprat and herring, silver darlings
(now by Profit threatened with extinction)
still give up their millions for our tables;
anchovy, pilchard (and its sardine young)
ladyfish and milkfish, moon-eyes, ox-eyes,
two hundred herring species all in all,
and each ten million fleeting miracles
pillaged by men and seagulls, constantly harried
by whales and porpoises, predaceous fish,
Neptune's uncountable silver treasure-chest.

What age was I when first I saw a trout
(taken from some lowland burn near Glasgow)
stippled black and red, a speckled wonder,
black through brown through yellow interchanging,
and was hooked on trout for life? Six or seven
or even less. And by the Allender later
many a boyhood Saturday, ill-equipped
with sixpenny rod, one fly, failed to catch one.
Then as schoolboy in St. Andrews caught my quota
of four- to eight-ouncers on the Lade Braes burn
(Kinness) and Kenly; by sixteen graduated
to the fighting pounders up on Cameron Loch,
and a Cairnsmill monster lost after ten minutes.
So to more recent times and my Linlithgow
best (five trout ten pounds in a couple of hours)
and my (best of all) five-pounder on the Tweed
yon day when, having failed to tempt a salmon,
I changed instead to a trout cast in the twilight.
The explosion when I struck, the breath-taking runs
ending in those frightening air-borne leaps –
once, twice, seven times he towered –
and then the dogged plunging round the net.
I who by that time had taken sea-trout
just as big, and a twenty-two pound salmon,
among a score of other fighting fish,
have never known a thrill like that big brownie.

How can I, you ask, be such a monster?
There you betray a common misconception,
for every man loves the thing he kills
(Wilde had the reality inverted)
and tribes make gods of the animals they feed on:
canibals devour their honoured foes:
a theological whale would worship krill:
and christians eat their God in their Communion.
Life has greater mysteries far than this.

But it is true my predatorial guilt
is steadily inhibiting the hunter,
though I can't deny my father Esau's nature
on pain of causing damage to the psyche:
but were I younger now I think I'd follow
those who wield the camera as weapon,
sublimating thus the hunter's urges.

Salmo salar, lord of the northern river
if not the sea, life's most beautiful emblem
(Mungo's fish of my once 'dear green' birthplace),
sockeye, humpback, quinnat, or our own
grilse and springers, autumn kipper and baggot, .
surging into the rivers intent on spawning –
who can see your leaps at weir or ladder,
heroic power pitted against the torrent,
and not feel moved as any epic poet
contemplating his hero's deeds of glory?
The spiral from the ovum to the parr,
the smolt at two years outward bound for the ocean,
returning grilse or springer, autumn kipper,
forging up the floods to spawning streamlets,
the spent kelt descending, gills gone lousy,
skinny of body, falling back to ocean,
mirrors the mighty spiral of evolution,
of water, of life, tight as a powerful spring
each coil curled close on its predecessor
as every year's a year but not the same year,
closely coiling round on the year before –
our heroic fable ritualised in the salmon.

See here this little ripple of clearest water
purling and wimpling over its gravelly bed,
liquid sunlight this October morning
on Teviot tributary, high above Hawick
(Scott country, home of our border clan
and I a Scott here visiting his homeland).
Look where that branch bows down there to the water –
do you not see that salmon and her mate,
the blue shadow paired by the larger red one
in water that can barely cover either,
that shallow spawning redd, their journey's end,
where tens of thousands eggs are to be laid
(ensuring two survive to replace the parents)
so that the coil of life goes on unhindered?
Who can witness that scene of generation
and not be moved by a religious awe,
a spell-bound sense of tender reverence for,
a worship of, this Mystery of Life?

So with the sea-trout and other salmon species,
each in its nature, brown trout and rainbow,
char and various whitefish, grayling, powan,
and the several species of vendaces:
brute power of spine in muscle sheathed.
And other fish of equal vertebrae –
the nightmare widemouths of the nether deeps
black as Satan or the Stygian pit
and decked with head and side lamps for that world
darker than darkest night: the mormyrids
of the Nile and other African rivers, some
with beak on chin to dig up bedded creatures.
O mighty arapaima of Brazil
and the Guianas, fifteen feet of power,
the heaviest of all freshwater fishes –
did He who made the stickleback make thee?
Ridiculous – the living God's no 'he'.

In waters that no salmonid could live in,
(Duddingston, Dunsappie in Edinburgh here,
ponds in the Vale of Health on Hampstead Heath)
there the green-striped pike, the spiv, is king,

a freshwater shark with little to fear but men,
leisurely lounging among his stagnant weeds
like gangster in dark alley or sad street corner,
devouring here and there a frog, an eel, his own young,
dragging down young water-hen or duckling
with Nature's cruel, indifferent approval –
hard to admire him. Let us move on
to his wee cousin the blackfish of Siberia
who can endure freezing a winter season
and thaw out spry as a goldfish in the spring.

(20)

Carnivorous characins that terrorize
Latin American, African lakes and rivers,
was it for your voracious massacres
that Life evolved the tools of spine and teeth?
That the tiger-fish, the 'water-dog' of Nile,
like some great pike, freshwater barracuda,
should gorge its four-foot length with lesser fishes?
That South America's piraña fish
ferociously should strip a luckless horse
or other animal, or man, to the bone
in a few minutes exposure to the pack?
A long way yet, the road to Calvary,
the hemlock, golden mean, or bo-tree shade.
Lucky Assisan with merely wolves to lecture!

Even the Spanish 'salmon' of La Plata,
the beautiful dorado, is no vegetarian
moonfish in diet but a beast of prey.
And what of those naked-backs, near allied,
in similar waters, lacking dorsal fins
like common eels, yet aren't eels but fish?
One of them we miscall electric eel:
but has life no better use for spines than shocking
poor pack-horses with five hundred volts
of fish-engendered electricity?

From all such carping let us turn to carps,
the fishiest fish, fifteen hundred species,
most numerous of all fish families
(our common carp, our roach, our chub, tench,
bream and whitebream, zope and zarthe
conspicuous to us at least among them)
scattered over all the continents
(saving Australia) though shunning America South
and its atrocious race of characins,
engaging creatures, whose teeth are embedded
not in their mouths but deep-set in their throats,
there arranged in rows on either side.

The carp kind is mostly rather gentle;
inoffensive little fishes, born
to line the stomachs of their predators:
yet king of them's the six-foot game mahseer,
lord of the Ganges and the Bramaputra,
conqueror of many a broken angler.
But the mahseer's not so typical of its kind
as our little friend the golden carp must be,
dressed by the Chinese and the Japanese
in glowing mandarin robes of rich design
to decorate our ponds, like the water-lilies.

Who would have thought these little hill-burn loaches
were pioneers in the move from gill to lung?
Yet how else reckon their gulping down of air
whenever their water gets too foul for breathing,
passing it through their intestinal tract
thus conscripted for purposes of breathing?

We Europeans with only a couple of catfish
out of sixteen hundred over the globe
associate them with that innocent world
of Tom Sawyer and Huckleberry Finn
in the not so innocent pages of Mark Twain.
Yet the biggest European freshwater fish,
the wels or glanis (they may scale four hundred pounds)
in rivers east of the Rhine, is one of the two,
unlovely creatures groping about in mud
with feeler-fingers underneath the chin
for the prey that swells its gross bulk out.

And in such bedded mud the eel's at home,
slippery-slithery insinuations of muscle
coiled round spine, swimming as serpents crawl,
a writhing progress of smooth and slimy wriggles
which, again like snakes, can ferry them
over land, through grass and vegetation
to reach a sea-going stream, when the mating call
draws them irresistibly down to ocean
and the long voyage to the Sargasso Sea,
then the climax of mating, spawning and death:

the elvers later taking the road back
to the streams and ponds their parents left to get them –
one of the most awesome miracles of Nature,
of her coiling, spiralling form of evolution.
Beside this mystical pilgrimage the conger,
moray, and other larger species of eel
are plain nuns compared to St. Teresa,
their lives to one, the lower, world confined:
not, like her, in one life at home in two.

How on Earth can the name of eel be given
to nightmare forms like thornback and gulper-eel?
Baffling knowledge, creatures of the abyss,
depths of inferno Dante never knew,
these midnight forms amaze the upper air,
the first an animated sawfish saw
with all the organ-systems of a fish,
the second a lash, a thick-hafted stock-whip
of which the haft is a fish of Stygian dark,
its mouth a needle-toothed maw that can devour
(like the anaconda), thicker prey than itself
and many times its own weight and volume.
Some of these creatures of eternal night
nevertheless pay homage to the Sun,
the principle of light, our heavenly sire,
by growing lanterns on their heads and sides
so that their element must often seem
like some pitch night of fireflies, will-o-the-wisps,
and meteors here and there in that inky sky.
Vast is your power O Sun, O lord of Life!

(21)

How different these tiny killifishes,
carp-toothed massacrers of insect larvae,
flat-headed pouters scurrying through the waters –
the millions-fish of sun-drenched Barbados
eating malaria in mosquito larvae.

Senorito swordfish of old Mexico
dressed to kill the plainer-garbed ladies,
quite the don, are you not, my long-tailed flasher,
cold of eye but a ballerino of wooers –
I tell you, mini sir, we see right through you.

Weird the adaptations Nature begets:
four-eyed fish, for seeing above and below
at the same time: sightless fish of caves
and subterranean streams can't see at all
but sense through their papillae every least
palpation in the water round about:
uncrowned kings in their country of the blind.
Gar-fish with needle-nebs the surface scouring:
half-beaks (like gar-fish) with only lower jaw:
flying-fish that glide above the waves,
little bolts of blue on fins like pinions
as often I have seen them, chased by dolphins.
Nature creates miracles or nothing:
only they to her are possible.

Innocuous as girls, those spikeless fish
the luscious family of cods, soft-finned
haddock, pollack, whiting, hake and ling,
a hundred and twenty species all in all
including one freshwater one, the burbot:
and of such fish I sing the humble cod,
praise his white-and-khaki-dappled skin,
he whose flesh these nearing sixty years
has often been digested into mine,
whose liver oil has saved so many lives,
nurtured uncountable children (me among them).
Incomputable our debt to this great fish

pursuit of whom by storm-tossed fishing heroes
led our kind to Greenland, Canada,
and all that mighty continent, 'these States'
that noble old Walt Whitman loved to sing –
How apt it is the name should rime with God
(to Whom alone the Boston Cabots talk).
I myself have fished or sprooled for them
in the Firth of Forth – and once when still a boy
taken by D'arcy Thompson to the Isle of May,
came home to St. Andrews late with a ten-pound cod
(which D'Arcy made the boatmen hand me over)
caught off the Isle while we were all ashore.
And I've caught codling from St. Andrews rocks
or off the pier while fishing for young saithe:
blessings on their single, pallid barbel.

Who ever named a fish a grenadier?
A rat-tailed fish that ramrod-spined parader?
Who called five hundred pounds of dumpling fish
a moon-fish, or opah (sounds more like
some instrument in a military band)?
Wonderful what may be done with spine –
the ribbon-fish their name identifies;
the oarfish from its pair of pelvic sculls;
the tube-fishes no tutor need explain;
the pipe-fish, in no sense secretive
though formed to be by certain seaweeds hidden;
but the sea-dragon only seems his name.

Rarest of all eccentrics of the seas
(rare in form I mean, not in number)
that upright water-fairy, the sea-horse
(no kelpie he) tail-anchored to a frond
as hitching-post, a delicate mirage,
some hyper-aesthete's too exquisite dream:
yet he's the little father hatching eggs
in secret pouch under that same tail.

(22)

I cannot think of D'Arcy and the sea
and all these far-off days through which
that outsized bearded figure strode like a god,
coat flying open, stetson on back of head,
the beautiful voice talking at fifty yards
and carrying a third or so of South Street,
without recalling the Bute and his museum
(where first he found me prowling round the cases)
with its entrance porch by local school-girls painted,
an under-water scene of cobalt blue
with fishes, eels and such in vivid colour:
and round the frieze above the walls and doorway
this legend even now fills me with awe –
They that go down to the sea in ships and do
business in the great waters, these men see
the works of the Lord, and His wonders in the mighty deep

So in this verse I too go down to the sea,
in the great waters see the works of the Lord
of Life, and his wonders in that mighty deep.

Unlike our soft-finned cods, the spike-finned fish,
soldier-fish, beryx (Alfonsino in Spain)
the pine-cone fish of Japan, John Dory,
all are armed with spike for defence and attack
fins with spiky, thorn-pointed ribs –
the thorn-points in some species poisoned.

The little six-barred perch of so many ponds
and rivers – who would guess how vast
the tribe of perches is, its families
various as the spoils of Aladdin's cave:
our predator perch may weigh five pounds or more
and strings the water with necklaces of eggs;
the little pope or ruffe of stagnant waters;
pike-perches, large as pike themselves;
tropical groupers, rock-fish, merous, hinds,
chameleons of the sea in their colour changes
to fit environs; various kinds of bass

including the five hundred pound black jewfish
fished for off the Californian coast;
snappers, grunts, Nile perches and robalos,
red mullet, surmullet and sea-breams,
Australian schnapper, the red tai of Japan
(emblem of Ebisa, the national fish-god),
various drums and roncadors or crackers,
squeteagues and the lordly maigre or meagre:
Australian trumpeters of eighty pounds,
blanquillos with their fey member the tilefish
all but extinguished in 1882
when millions corpses covered half the Atlantic;
the archer-fish, shooting water-arrows
at insects on the wing or trailing bough;
bristle-toothed butterfly fish, surrealist painter's
dream haunting the lanes of coral reefs
where they poke their snouts in holes for shrimp and such;
surgeon-fish or tangs with their lancet tails;
yellow-tail, scad, pilot-fish and dolphin,
iridescent sea-hounds coursing flying-fish;
blue-fish packs, those terrible wolves of the sea,
heavy as salmon, destructive as Tartar horde
devasting all that they encounter;
the numerous clan of wrasses building weed nests;
parrot-fishes with their polly beaks
browsing on the submarine weed-meadows;
cichlid perches of Africa, Brazil,
six hundred species (more or less) are known
(a hundred found in Tanganyika only);
angel-fish, and poison-spike-finned weevers,
dragonets, those submarine chimaeras –
the perches are a truly catholic race.
Most interesting of all, the climbing perch,
is not a perch at all, as analysts see it
but one of the allied labyrinthine fishes
equipped with a rosette lung as well as gills
enabling it to crawl about on land,
to climb low trees upon their spiny fins
and thus anticipate the amphibians,
as amphibians do reptiles, reptiles birds,
birds mammals, and certain mammals man –

not only trees the climbing perch ascends
but also this vast Tree of evolution.
The conquest of land by animals with spines
with them is on the way – but not yet come.

So many other fish of interest and wonder
no such foreshadowing show – the grey mullets,
barracudas (dangerous as sharks)
blancos, pescadors and silversides,
thread-fins, hair-tails, cutlass- and scabbard-fish,
the snoek, the mackerel clan including tuna
bonito, albacore, swordfish, sailfish,
snake-mackerels (gempylus) boarded Kon-tiki;
blennies and gobies of our own tidal pools
(with mangrove mud-skippers also raiding land)
and the sea-cat or wolf-fish (lush on the table)
shannies and butter-fish, the eel pout
(that brings forth alive its two-inch young),
the Cuban blind-fish and, strangest of all,
fierasfer, that smooth and shiny fishling
lives in the anus of the sea-cucumber
(a little whip-like darter who, when outside,
knocks his host on the nose for returned entry)
weirdest, surely, of all weird partnerships.
Fish with cheeks of mail like the gurnard sept,
rock perch, scorpion-fish and lion-fish,
poison-fish, sea-robins, horsefish, greenlings,
miller's thumbs and (spare us!) father-lashers,
lumpsuckers, armoured bullheads, sticklebacks
(daddy builds the nest, brings up the young),
dragon fish and remoras (those hobos
and hitch-hikers of the seas are used,
tied on rope, to take turtles captive).

And what of the down-trodden, tramped-on flatfish,
deformed sports with wry one-sided eyes?
I've never shared the taste for sole or dab,
flounder, plaice or brill, nor lemon sole
(though I enjoy the halibut and turbot).
And what of all those join-jawed poisonous fish
that cause such dread disease as ciguatera?

Or the trigger-fishes (one comes near to England)
file-fish, trunk-fish, cow-fish and puffers,
the huge oceanic sun-fish, all vast head;
the porcupine or burr-fish, aptly named;
cling-fishes, spine-eels, toad- and angler-fish
(whose luscious tails are sold as monk or 'dory'),
fishing-frog, the horny deep-sea angler
with tiny male a fin-like fixed appendage
under the female's large and negroid bulk,
often a thousand times as big's her spouse.

Of all the fishes ever swam the sea,
some of great beauty and nobility,
surely mud-fish are the least appealing?
Yet it's the mud-fish, not tarpon or salmon,
that pioneers (with other humble fish)
the vertebrate take-over of the land:
rude forefathers of the amphibians.

With air-bladders transforming into lungs
(entirely replacing gills in times of drought)
these lung-fish, all these double-breathers
tottering on the cliff-edge of extinction,
yet pioneered the land for lizards, mammals:
the lobe-finned coelacanth long thought extinct
but still equipped for an amphibious life:
the barramundi of Queensland, gulping air;
the mud-fish of Brazil and Africa
surviving in mud like buried saintly gurus,
in desert dying in neither land nor sea –
the moon has felt the tread of their progeny.

(23)

The double-sided life on land and water
many and various kinds of creature live –
snakes and crocodiles, penguins, otters, beavers,
seals and sea-lions as well as fish we've noticed –
is not the same as true amphibians,
frogs and toads, newts and salamanders
who almost all begin life in water,
only later developing legs and lungs –
all a halfway house to reptiles, birds and mammals.

Froggie would a-wooin' go, ha-ha!
but the frog is no anthropomorphic joke
from folk-song or from Aesop – here indeed
we find a true near-image of mankind
if not of all our dryland vertebrates.
No fish has arms and legs, hands and feet
with fingers and toes like ours, fore and upper arms,
thighs and shins, a skeleton much like ours,
a musculature similar to ours,
biceps and triceps, deltoids and pectorals,
a spine and brain much like the human brain,
a nervous system served by eyes and ears,
a nose, a tongue, a dank but sensitive skin
and glandular system not unlike our own,
a well-developed alimentary tract,
a chambered heart and double blood system
with all the usual arteries, veins and such.
Above all, he has lungs (though only used
when emergencies demand more oxygen
than skin and buccal membranes can supply)
and a vocal box like Caruso (though less tuneful).
Add to that a brace of fertile testes
and no wonder Froggie (as near the image of man
as man is the image of God) would a-wooin' go.

Nor all the other frogs and amphibians
living and extinct: the Coal Age roofheads
Darwinian ancestor-worshippers think our sire:
the legless coecilians burrowing in the soil,

the newts and salamanders tailed with rudders:
tiger-salamanders often arrested
at their adult tadpole stage as axolotls
breeding and begetting axolotls
in anti-neotenic sad regression
as many of the genera seem to do –
permanently gilled adolescents
(olms, mud-eels and many other species):
the many true and tailless frogs and toads,
the jumpers which outnumber all these others,
with five-toed feet and four-fingered hands
and the physiology outlined above.

Slender Mr Frog in his svelte green coat
mottled and dappled here and there, or spotted:
squat Mr Toad with horny-warty skin
that got him, in the folk-mind, linked with the Devil:
they and their tadpoles people a boy's world
even in and around the largest cities
(I myself bred frogs from spawn in Glasgow):
frogs for the tables of French and other gourmets
(brekekekex, the Aristophanic frogs,
tragic bards, and Euripides' 'wee hip flask'):
hairy frogs, bull-frogs, Cameroon goliaths
big as terriers, eating full-grown rats.

How well I remember ju-ju nights in Lagos
along the Marina, past King George's Park,
moonlight magicking the suave lagoon,
the asterisk palm-trees dark against the sky,
a million crickets rehearsing their simple song,
the basso-profundo bull-frogs in the mangroves
quorking a litany lacks all parts but the bass;
and from the mainland dark across the lagoon
Yoruba voices chanting their timeless songs;
and the sands rattle-rustling with scuttling crabs
at my approach – all the air was full
(as in a cathedral vast beyond men's dreams)
of the indescribable presence of Nature's God,
the holy spirit of our beloved Earth
at one with her beautiful daughter, Africa,

vibrant, rare, intangible, real as air
and as invisible, old as time and yet
young as the future, indeed outside of time,
that world my whole roused being wholly adored,
the creature's ardent love of its Creator.

Burrowing frogs and flying frogs, frogs
that climb up trees; paradoxical frogs
which grow not up but down, their ten-inch tadpoles
ending as one-inch frogs; frogs with horns
and frogs whose poison tips the Indian's arrow;
tree-frogs hatching their young upon their backs;
African plat-handers with no tongues.
Are not we all, like them, between two worlds
poised, pulled by both, quite at home in neither?

The humbler toad with his repulsive skin
dry as matting, wartier than Cromwell,
often as podgy as some complacent bourgeois
bloated and paunchy with ill-gotten grub,
cuts no such lover figure as masher frog.
Yet he too must share dalliance with the gods
and dance to the tunes of Eros and Aphrodite,
clasping a mate no lovelier than himself.
Bufo (the buffoon?) the Romans called him:
but are not humans only, in all Creation,
love's clowns? Where among toads
can you find the peers of Romeo and Juan,
Solomon (Sheba's fool, and many others'),
Anthony, who for lust well lost his world;
poor outraged Abelard and his Heloise;
Dido, on whose pyre all Carthage burned
to slake the savage lust of brute Rome;
Orpheus himself whose tom-cat wails of desire
turned into music charmed the queenly spheres,
the whole Creation, and even Hell itself?
What Villon toad beneath his Katherine's window
lost his skin beneath the hangman's lash?
What female toad, instead of stringing spawn
around her sensible reeds played Ophelia
drowned between two loyalties of love?
Bufo be to those who bufo think!

(24)

The reptiles come in salamander shape
or newt, or even worm, the animals
that crawl (the name implies) though few of them
(these scaly and cold-blooded vertebrates)
but the snake and such are aptly so described:
but they are not amphibious, never know
a tadpole childhood, gilled for submarine breathing.
Worshippers of ancestors (and Darwin)
tell us that of course they are derived
from such forms as newts, as we all are from the One
Pan-Ancestor, denying evolution
its obvious and vast creative power –
harmless twaddle unless you should mistake
a crocodile for an outsize salamander.

Put it another way – the tadpole stage
in post-amphibian forms (including human)
is spent in the womb-egg's amniotic fluid –
a must invention for all spinal species
freeing themselves from water for land and air –
yet breathing through the tail, the allantois.
The reptile's egg cradled the first land beast
and colonised the land and upper air,
making the post-coal age a reptile one
(though birds and mammals too were plentiful):
and of those reptiles lizards kinged the castle,
saurians of a myriad myriad forms
(aquatic, airborne, land, tree, burrowing)
that had their dog-day (how many million years?)
then disappeared, or shrunk to our mere lizards.
The kings of the Earth are but ephemeral.

Where now are those great monarchs used to be?
Ichthyosaur, ambelodon, archelon,
the rhamphorhyncus and tyrannosaurus,
iguanodon, diplodocus, brontosaurus
and countless other Lost World potentates
now to us a legion of ponderous names?
Mais ou son les dinosaurs d'antan?

Precisely where les neiges d'antan are gone
(although it must be said they left more traces).
One of them stands out above all others
by pioneering vertebrates in air;
the finger-winged flying lizard, pterodactyl –
not to be confused with earliest birds
but a reptile of the reptiles, though airborne.

Here the fable takes us to New Zealand
where snout-headed tuatara (sphenodon) lives
a (so science tells us) living fossil
like coelacanth and other 'fossils' living,
survivor, it is said, of the Age of Reptiles,
with its pineal eye atop its head.
Spine ridged with spikes against predation,
wide-mouthed head somehow like Bertrand Russell
seen in profile, tuatara looks
from his philosopher's eye as one whose gaze
has seen it all, an unimpressible yogi
freed from the Wheel, the coil of evolution,
comprehending a million million years
in each casual momentary glance,
like some old god preceded Maui-tiki:
an age-old watchman keeping an eye on things.

Rolling down through all the rocky ages
(see yuh later alligator: in a while crocodile)
the deathless line of crocodilia
grinning through their crocodilian tears
creeps through twentieth-century swamps and rivers,
has seen the inscrutable sphinxes come and go
and are as like to see the human race
(we who pack our vanities in their hides).
Humble enough their niche, their branch of the Tree,
but like so many unheroic species
life-tenacious, surviving many fitter,
surprising in their mean variety:
South American crocodiles or caimans
no bigger than our local pike or salmon;
thirty-foot or so sea crocodile
swimming hundreds of miles between sea islands

(Fiji to the Solomons for instance);
fish-eating gharials with gar-like noses;
the crocodile of destiny on the Nile
burying its eggs in layers down in sand holes;
long-snout crocodiles of Africa
where I have seen them on the lordly Niger;
the alligators of the Mississippi;
muggers of the Ganges and Bramaputra;
the jumbucks of Matilda's billabong;
a horny, gnashing, lash-tailed, stone-eyed race
which, more than any creatures I can think of,
astonish me that we should share the Earth with.

(25)

What poet in the guise of scientist
named 'chelonia' tortoises and turtles?
You'd think that they were birds of paradise
not lumbering plated tanks on wooden legs
(instead of revolving caterpillar tracks)
like the Aldebran tortoise, loggerhead turtle.

He who lives by the shell dies by the shell
and sorely these brutes pay for their defence,
entombed alive in their own carapaces,
living mausoleums of themselves
without mobile ribs to help their breathing,
opportunities for further adapting:
like sad neurotics wearing the rut they're stuck in
for sometimes far too long a martyrdom
(a tortoise Cook gave Tonga only died
some years ago in nineteen sixty-six:
Marian's tortoise died at a hundred and sixty).

Alligator-snappers of Missouri-Mississippi
luring their prey (by artificial bait
in their mouths) literally into the jaws of death;
small musk-turtles of North Americas
popularly known as stink-pot terrapins;
true tortoises; painted; diamond-backed;
red-eared, wood and slider terrapins
grown for the table and acquaria
(some of them), box-turtles, the giant tortoise
of Galapagos, Seychelles and other islands
(sometimes scaling almost a thousand pounds)
once providing meat on the hoof for sailors
so that the species soon were all but extinguished;
the also giant African spurred tortoise
and many smaller breeds, including burrowers
like the North American gopher-tortoises.

These ocean-wandering argonauts, the turtles,
coming ashore only to lay their eggs,
lumbering up the coral sands and beaches

chased by sharks and watched by pirate birds
to scoop out holes in sand to plot their eggs in
before lumbering back to the sea and the sharks
and whatever fate: green turtle, hawksbill,
loggerhead and Ridley's: leaving their young
to hatch out later by many moons and alone
find their own way down to their mother ocean,
preyed on by sea-birds, vultures, crabs and animals,
and the fish await the few who reach the water –
Nature red indeed in beak and claw,
obedient to its own law of predation.
So with their eccentric second cousins
the luths or leathery turtles, not horn-plated,
at eight feet largest of all and near a ton:
stream-lined argos of the Pacific ocean
with speeds of over twenty miles per hour;
they too endure the trials of the sea.

(26)

If tortoises and turtles could escape
the plated prison of their carapaces
they would become so many kinds of lizard:
aristocratic reptiles of long descent
from their mighty ancestors who ruled the Earth
(if 'ruled' is not a monstrous humanism)
the dinosaurs of the so-called Age of Reptiles.

Twenty-five thousand living lizard species
neighbour mankind on the Earth to-day;
aquatic lizards, burrowing, even gliding
(not truly flying as pterodactyls did)
from chasm to snowpeak, desert to densest jungle
(these cold-blooded creatures favour the tropics),
some running, some crawling, some snakelike winding,
all or almost all on insects feeding.

The smallest lizard alive is a Virgin Island
gecko, measuring less than an inch and a half;
and I recall the green geckos in Lagos
running across the ceiling upside down
(some fall on necks and floor and scamper off)
and aground the lizards green, blue and orange
(by accident tramp on the tail and it comes off).
The skink I don't recall, commonest lizard,
their order's Tuaregs in scorching desert
swimming through hot sand as if through water –
the desert's fish, as the camel is its ship.

Lacertidae, the Romans named the lizards
common enough in their sun-pampered land,
the green lizard bobs in Pompeii ruins;
common and sand lizard; the eyed, the thorn-fingered,
look on life with stoical disdain:
American teguexin, striped like a long-tailed tabby;
the Amazon's herbivorous dracaena
(race-runners of its sandier regions)
and lesser cousins with eyelid window-panes
(creatures unable to shut their eyes to things)

skimble and scamble about in lizard fashion:
those two-way goers (*amphisbaenidae*)
with tails so like their heads you can't tell which
is which as they, sans eyes, ears, even limbs,
indifferently head or tail first, burrow
through subterranean tubes, like tube-locos.
The mind is stunned by life's varieties.
See largest lizards, goannas or monitors
with snaky tongues and tails, Komodo Dragon
chief among them, ten-foot long three hundred
pound devourer of small wild pigs and such:
the Indian bis-cobra, kabara goya,
often so mistaken for poisonous –
and that West African monitor shamming dead!
American Gila monsters and beaded-lizards
(really the only poisonous ones)
eating their lesser kin in desert places,
while snakelike slow-worm types in Australian airts
are harmless hide-aways among the grasses;
and glass-snakes, scheltopusik of Morocco,
American snake-lizards (*anguidae*)
and our slow-worm of diffident grassy places
(bringing forth their young in August),
girdled-lizards of Africa, Madagascar,
however they may look, are fierce as kittens.

Marine iguanas of the Galapagos
(the Tortoise Isles), blunt-snouted seaweed eaters
able to live an hour below the waves
(uniquely, among lizards, maritime)
upstage the green iguanas of the land
and all their kin; tree-climbing basilisks
with scale-fringed toes for petering on water
and cockscomb crest running from head to tail;
American 'chamaeleons' (*anales*)
which, like their namesakes change their colour;
horned-toads (so-called) of Mexican deserts
that squirt from their eyes jets of blood when scared,
and all their old-world kin, the agamids:
Australian moloch-lizards (thorny devils)
bearded lizards, the frilled chlamydosaur

which ruffs its frills to scare off enemies,
the burrowing mastigures of Africa,
the Indo-Burmese bloodsuckers (misnamed),
even perhaps its aerial opposite number
the flying-lizard of Malaysia
which glides from branch to branch or to the ground
on vans of skin umbrella-stretched on ribs
collapsible and folded when not in flight:
all these in heaven and earth, Horatio!

We humans have maligned the true chamaeleon
by using it to symbolise our twisters,
turncoat politicians, Vicar-of-Brays,
as George Buchanan did of Lethington
(whose poems would outweigh his many faults):
and as by this abusage we degrade
the lizard, so we flatter the turncoats.
These little creatures, masters of camouflage,
by life's authority but shift to live,
not driven by lust for power, envy or greed
or other sins assail less simple souls.
They fill their singular niche in many parts,
in Madagascar, Africa, Ceylon,
the genus holding many different species
(Madagascar alone has thirty-six)
but all with independently moving eyes,
prehensile tails to grasp the branches with,
a long and lightning-rapid sticky tongue:
the colour-changing they're so famous for
they share in fact with many lizard kinds.

(27)

The snake has long found favour with the Muse,
been made in our time great by D. H. Lawrence
(who shouldn't have left this Tree to my poor hands),
played its major role in Genesis,
been honoured by no less than Milton's pen
and other pens so greater far than mine.
Whence ascend two thousand serpent species
sliding and coiling, winding about the Earth?
The record of the rocks tells us but little
but does suggest a lizard-like beginning.
Did then the neotenic law obtain,
some lizard born with no (or too weak) legs
writhe forth on the road led to the anaconda,
reticulated python, the king cobra?
No lizard so enthralls imagination,
for evolution itself's an endless snake
coiling tightly round upon itself,
and the lower (legless) form's in fact the 'higher'
(silly term, but certainly the later),
still having 'feet' enough (in its underplates)
to catch on the ground and help to push forward
this most sensitive-tongued of spinal creatures.

Sensitive, they're secretive and timid
as Lawrence found on that glad day for poetry
when his water-trough was honoured by the viper
and he betrayed the fellowship of Nature.
Many snakes in certain ways are gentle,
fit pets for Arab and Indian charmers,
dancing to their tunes as our electorates
(changing sides in the game of snakes and charmers)
dance to the tunes of our no less venomous masters.

Least in snake society these blind ones are,
burrowing like worms, all head and tail,
so many species quite innocuous:
the South American ilysia
who imitates the venomous coral-snake,
threatening enemies with colossal bluff;

grass-snakes (living here in Britain),
slug-eating dipsads common in the tropics,
egg-eating dasypelts of Africa,
viperine-snakes of Spain and Southern Europe,
American moccasins, Indian keelbacks,
rat-snakes, garter-snakes and chicken-snakes,
the English smooth-snake (often misthought an adder) –
all harmless as far's mankind's concerned,
like many other of their humble kind.

How different the veldt boomslang, and other
back-fanged poisonous snakes, although
for humans and other animals of size
the fangs are too far back to reach the flesh
injecting there their blood-destroying venom
(though none but fools would take a chance on it).
But front-fanged species like the Indian cobra
are nearly all death in the garb of snakeskin.
Some have poison acts by paralysing;
that of others destroys the blood corpuscles;
and some, like the Australian tiger-snake,
with one bite could kill a herd of cattle
or a flock of near four hundred adult sheep;
black snakes and death-adders are near as bad.
Your Indian king-cobra or hamadryad,
and many cobra kinds, don't need to bite
but merely spit their venom at your eyes.

At Tarquah Bay (near Lagos) I recall
a green mamba, as I was walking over
the coarse lianas trellising the sand
between the tree and shore lines, sprang to life
and fled, with the swishing sound of gushing water.
Eager to see it better, I chased after
on bare feet, but it outdistanced me.
And I have seen a Hausa entertainer
play with a black mamba like a pet.
One day at Ilorin, too, I mind
I left the camp to walk down to the river
through grass grew ever taller up around me
till my feet were out of sight in grass and water,

and at almost every step some snake or such
started away with spine-shivering rustle,
and pins and needles tingled under my scalp:
a great relief it was to reach that river
and find a well-trod path to bring me back.
And in Pompeii once among the ruins
a viper I startled franticly rushed about,
poking at the far wall of the ruined house,
till a tiny hole sucked in his two-foot length.

Front-fanged bungarus of India;
the yellow-black-red banded coral snakes
(the real and deadly ones) of America;
the sea-snakes of Pacific and Indian Oceans
(paddle-tailed with nostrils high on the nose)
that instead of eggs bring forth their young alive;
and all the clan of rattlesnakes and vipers
(the rattles helped them escape the bison hooves),
diamond-back, sidewinder, prairie rattler,
African puff-adders five feet long,
horned and Gaboon vipers, our own adder
and her Indian cousin the dabaia;
pit vipers of America and Asia,
cotton-mouths, copperheads, the dread bushmaster
(twelve feet in length) who khans the prairie;
the jararaca, fer-de-lance and others,
all make Medusa's head seem flossy-bunny
compared to their coiled panoply of terror.

Less dangerous to man are the constrictors,
often noble creatures and beautiful
of colour and design, boas of the New World,
pythons of the Old, crushing to death their prey
(birds and small deer, rodents, pigs
narrow enough for them to swallow whole):
boa constrictors less than a dozen feet
would probably find a terrier too big,
as most of the many kinds of python would.
But even the mighty giants of the family,
the anaconda of Amazon and its forests
(as much at home in the river as in trees),

reticulated python of south-east Asia
(the wise old Kaa of Kipling's Jungle Book)
scarce could swallow even a half-grown pig.
Yet it's in them we find the spine of bone
most perfectly and solely incarnated,
sans arms, sans legs or other appendages
of which the birds and mammals make such use.

(28)

Ave, Aves, of animals A per se!
So I thought in boyhood anyway
writing on pet goldfinch my first poem
in Glasgow where I haunted all the pet shops
selling finches, linnets, redpolls, siskins
(as well as love-birds, budgies and canaries),
and the Art Gallery's ornithological cases
full of stuffed birds from the wild world,
and pored over bird-books instead of doing homework.
Then St. Andrews, where I was myself
like a cage-bred wild bird suddenly set free
in a wonder-world to which I was at once
both a native and yet bred a stranger,
a world in which so many birds till then
never seen alive, flew in the flesh –
experiences I hoarded like a miser
or one who stumbles on a pirate's treasure.

Birds are the poets of the animal world,
glorified lizards (but at times *such* glory!).
How did the Life-artist's teeming genius
create feathers out of lizard scales?
From grunts and croaks the song of nightingale,
of lark and bulbul, wren and campañero?
Or is this more Darwinian misconception?
Yet there's the archaeopteryx with its teeth,
lizard-like tail, and fingers tipped with claws,
distinctly reptile like the pterodactyl
yet (unlike it) also a crow-sized bird;
although in flight no swift or albatross,
its keel too weak to bear strong flying muscles,
probably just flapping from tree to tree.
Those later (long-gone) birds the ichthyornis
(gull-like diving for its fish at sea)
and hesperornis (flippered like the penguins)
seem to be less lizard-like in frame.
Who knows how many thousand species died
and left no trace that they had ever been
save (unknown) in birds alive to-day?

Great auk, dodo, solitaire, passenger pigeon –
leaves from the Tree we have no knowledge of.

Birds as we know them, searching out (it seems)
all that the new bone skeleton can achieve
with wings (using feather as well as skin),
from the bee-like humming-bird to the soaring condor,
including those (like the kiwi) abandoned wings
or (like the penguins) abused them as fins.
Begin with the ostrich-types, the 'ancient jaws'
(so the ornithologists aver,
these Sherlock Holmeses of anatomy),
strangely almost all a flightless clan.
Here the extinct forms too take precedence,
the aepyornis (Sindbad the Sailor's roc?)
and those great moas done to death by Maori
not long after Tasman found New Zealand.
But the longest pedigreed living are the emu
species (two), native to Australia,
tailless birds, like all but two of the clan,
with double feathers (as in forms extinct) –
one outer, one the inner nestling down.
Evening and morning on their sandy plains
or sparse woodlands, emus forage roots,
grass and fruit, and bathe (if there's a creek):
swift escapers, fighters with a kick
and booming, noisy lovers in mating season.
Despite its average ten green eggs,
sheep farmers menace this soul with extinction,
fencing off the water it depends on:
one species may be extinct already.

Better in adaptation, the cassowary
is something of an artist in coloured plumage,
skin of head and neck, in all twenty species –
scarlet, yellow, blue and indigo
with lappets often hanging from the checks –
and a more dangerous (forward-kicking) fighter,
whether in Australia or nearby islands
charging through the heavy bush or jungle
with helmeted head, at thirty miles per hour:

a lethal pet for bushmen who would tame them
(gralloching a man with one spiked kick)
the female larger and more dangerous
(though the male alone tends the eggs and young).

Creatures of the eye, not nose or feelers,
birds are sensitive to light and colour
(much of their behaviour due to light)
their plumage a living painterly aesthetic.
Daintiness of foot they seem to favour
paring to four the five toes of the lizard
(or to only three in emu and cassowary,
or in the ostrich only one and a bit).
So with the lesser ostrich of the pampas
the harem-running rhea, sport of the gaucho,
companion of the guanaco and the deer,
its one-toed hoof is made for such terrain
(the toes seem to be closing in a hoof);
its plumage of a smoky-bluish grey
(so Hudson tells us) merges in the haze –
a useful attribute for the rhea father
hatching his wives' four dozen eggs to a nest.

But lord of all this clan, the African ostrich
roaming the sandy plains with herds of zebra
antelope, gazelle and other deer,
eight-foot eccentric teacher staring down on
the class of midget pupils who affront him,
pin head poised on a scrawny chimney stack
rearing out of his sable morning coat –
but look, teacher's got no trousers on!
So I myself, out one day in Kaduna
(Bukuru was it? Jos? I've forgotten)
cycling sharply round a slummy corner
nearly ran bang into this grotesque
(and just as nearly fell back off the saddle).
The gaunt apparition merely stared
(no, not at all a delirium tremens case
but simply one of truth stranger than fiction).

The dowdier female ostriches take turns

of brooding, blending with the ground by day:
the male (who rolls his sable wings in courtship)
is better dressed to suit the negro night.

This ostrich clan has curious septs and branches:
kiwis are kin, with their compatriot moa
though these myopic, Pecksniffian nosers
(wingless, weak and vulnerable too)
survive the moa (dead two hundred years),
nostrils on their beak-tips for the purpose
sensitively sniffing the ground for worms
or grubs, beetles and other suchlike sweets
moving in the rich New Zealand night.
Kiwi wears his penis outwardly
and his happy spouse lays an enormous egg
deep in their burrow under some tree's roots
for her spouse happily to incubate.
Kiwis also pack a terrific kick,
enough to slash a dog in to the bone.
The clan as kin claims also tinamous
(though I'd have thought the game birds' claim is better)
from Patagonia up to Mexico
the thirty-three known species, powerful fliers,
seem unlikely classed with ostriches:
guinea-fowl, more like, to my lay eyes,
or even argus pheasants wanting the tail.
Indeed, the rufescent kind was tried in England
as gun-fodder, but luckily failed the test;
so in the wild it still lays beautiful eggs
(multi-coloured and glossy as porcelain)
like all the other species of its kind
prowling the undergrowth of bush and forest
or open pampas of Latin America.
They too leave uprearing to the male,
explosive in flight and brief as flying fish,
their heavy bodies easily tire the wings:
yet some are found in the upper heights of Andes
feeding mainly on insects, vegetation.
Some are small, no bigger than a quail,
others big as any barnyard rooster:
but all have come a long way from the ocean.

(29)

These grounded forms, most basic among birds,
are also the least typical, and pose
a paradoxical problem about flight –
the readiness of birds to give it up
whenever the choice is less than life or death.
Who would pinions bear, to labour long
under a weary wing, keeping aloft
a heavy body against strong gravity
(and sometimes stronger winds in all weathers)
save the alternative were death aground:
when like the dodo, emu or the moa
he might himself relax in bush or plain
unconstrained to labour up the sky?
The bones of such beachcombers grave time's beaches.

So (among 'new jaws' of this clan) the divers
use their wings for swimming more than flying,
and hesperornis's direct descendants,
penguins, have regressed to ancestral fins,
flying after fish in a sky of sea
(as falcon after dove in a sea of sky)
on flipper wings, with paddle-feet astern.

My first meeting with those beautiful birds
was in St. Andrews, a great northern diver
oiled-up near Dhu Craig, sailed straight to my hand
as if he knew I was his only hope
and trusted me to save him from his fate.
Alas for his trust! I took him down to D'Arcy
at the Bute, but though we tried our best
with chemicals whose names I now forget,
the case was hopeless and the bird declined
till I with ether ended his misery
(and began my own for having failed that trust).
Out of that sting and similar ones felt since
I learned Man's place in Nature's universe:
to be as good a shepherd as he may
to all his fellow-creatures on the Earth
(what though he slaughter some at times to live).

Red-throated divers and black-throated ones

have wintered near my windows on the Prom
here in Portobello on the Forth,
porpoising from the rollers in their dives,
lying so low little but heads were showing.
But the white-billed diver keeps to harsher climes:
why should these creatures and so many others
choose to live in the hell of polar regions?
Are they freer there from larger predators,
or is food more plentiful, easier to get?
Necessity, be sure, that stern mother
forces them to such ascetic virtue
(though their cries sound more like demons than like saints.

Most beautiful of all rump-footed birds
the eighteen grebes are surely ugliest named.
What's 'to grebe', perdee, what chunder-headed
grasping, toe-handed oaf of a French farmer
dubbed these ballerinas such a title?
I've seen the nuptial pas-de-deux of two
great-crested ones, standing on the water,
shaking beaks and ruffs each at other,
dancing away then back again – ye gods,
the Panovs couldn't choreograph their dance!
See their dives to bring some weed-stalks up
to show each other in their bustling flurry
before they build their raft-like, floating nest
that can rise or fall with the water level:
for those birds are as fond of lochs and rivers
as their diver cousins are of the open sea.
What other birds, when danger menaces,
can dive with all their chicks upon their backs?
What bird other than the little pied-bill grebe
can boast as many as fifteen thousand feathers?
Their plumage nearly brought extinction to
some species in the feather-wearing age:
the great-crested with its Tudor frills for instance,
like others, has been hunted near to death.
But still the dabchick, the horned (Slavonian) grebe
the red-necked, black-necked, and western ones survive:
and high in the Andes, above twelve thousand feet,
the flightless grebe Lake Titicaca graces,
as does the Atitlan grebe the Atitlan Lake.

(30)

Did Charlie Chaplin imitate the penguins,
or are penguins his unconscious understudies?
Spheniscidae, the bird men quaintly call them,
but originally 'penguin' meant 'great auk'
(the late great) but somehow got transferred
to this flippered clan of sixteen septs or so,
all satirists of sentries and of butlers,
but like all birds with well-developed hearts
to keep the blood-warmth well above the mammal:
how else thrive in their Antarctic hell?

How *do* they thrive? Many of them don't,
but make Darwin's 'natural selection'
(the mode of biological adaptation)
look gey thin. Take the emperor penguin
whose young hatch out in twenty-four hour night
with almost eighty per cent mortality,
much of it through chicks being torn to bits
(Solomon's wisdom never heard of here)
between parents and others (bereaved of their own)
grabbing for solace at any neighbour's chick:
behaviour consonant with the darkest night.
Yet these three-foot eighty pound galoots
can hatch their chicks at seventy-eight below,
the male mainly, in a two-month fast, brooding
(the only time he leaves the icy seas),
and those chicks do survive are old enough
to face alone their own first total night,
slat-winged little heroes, confronting fate.

Next, in this quaint aristocracy
of birds, to the emperor there comes the king
(hatching the egg in his abdominal pocket),
king of Patagonia and such places
(Kerguelen, New Zealand, Tasmania and South Georgia).
Other penguins sport less snobbish names:
rock-hopper, Adelie, the jackass even,
macaroni, the yellow-eyed, the blue
(puffin-sized busty pygmy of the clan),

the Snares crested, and the Galapagos
(the only one to settle in the tropics);
some of them scaling heights like mountaineers;
most can waddle miles from sea to nest
and back again, tobogganing down bergs;
rock-hoppers bounce along like kangaroos;
all of them beautiful and appealing birds,
whether the little Charlies (like the blue)
or the big de Gaulles (like the king and emperor)
strutting, long neb indicating heaven,
arched-out longbow front strung on the spine,
feet out of sight of their own eyes,
world-vision distinctly de haut en bas.

(31)

Ocean, thou mighty element of water
from whom all animated beings rise
to whom all living things return,
what pen, what mind, what soul can ever sing
in praise the terror, glory, of your divine
wonders, miracles of living art?
What trumpet voice can adequately sing
a song does justice to your majesty?
Not even Melville, Conrad, mighty bards
who loved and sailed on you, your true poets,
can other than but hint at your vast being,
mother who bears only heroic sons.

Yet no man ever born can emulate
the storm-petrel, water-walking Peter,
who nestles on the bosom of your tempests
as lesser mortals doze on feather-beds,
plucks his living from the jaws of savage waves
(in weathers that would daunt an eskimo),
true child of ocean, to ocean only true,
the storm's jockey, midget charged with power,
triumphing over impossibilities –
he and all his kin, from his six-inch self
up to the lordly wandering albatross
whose twelve-foot wing-span covers half the world,
are mysteries who with mysteries commune.

Mother Carey's chicken, the sailors dubbed
this little Peter walking the storm waves,
whose game of life and death with the turbulent ocean
made hir seem her spiritual emblem,
dark and foreboding as the storm's gurl,
musky and smelly, shooting rank oil at foes
(like all hir kind) through the gun-barrel clamped on hir bill
if molested when nesting, hatching the one white egg
in a rock-crevice, or the end of some burrow,
hiding by day, mistrusting the alien land.

Petrels exhaust the possibilities

of oceanic flight, as Chopin those of the piano,
Bach of the organ, Dante and Shakespeare of verse –
Wilson's petrel, most numerous of birds;
Leach's pintado, broad-billed blue, the giant
Nelly (near as big as the albatross);
the Manx shearwater (those swifts of the high seas),
wedge-tailed, little, and sooty shearwaters, the giant
(nesting on snoring Tristan's rocky bulk);
fulmar gliding silent on surf-board wings;
the diving petrel of down-under waters,
fifty-three species, more or less, in all;
all prodigies of flight as adaptation
(in that as far from ostriches as can be)
yet structurally seem quite primitive birds.
How can the young of some such birds, deserted
before they leave the nest, tumble from cliffs
and migrate thousands (unguided) miles to parents?
Such mysteries in birds are common-place,
as in eels and salmon and other migrant fish;
some insects make such mysteries seem plain.

But in the end this realm of flight belongs
to its true king, the maestro di maestri,
the wandering albatross who on lath-like wings
glides on the wind as if the wind were wings
that carry him by their, not his, exertion
over tens of thousands miles of untamed ocean,
living, eating, sleeping on the wing,
exile his home, and our home (land) where this
mighty lord of flight is gauche, his exile.
Those clever men who classify the birds
in Greek and Latin terms entitle him
the 'exiled Diomedes', that great hero
(coupled with Ulysses) served at Troy
and, nearly slain on return (like Agamemnon)
by the whore his wife, chose perpetual exile
in preference to such a life at home:
rumour has it he and his loyal men
were changed to albatrosses after death –
whence they are known as Diomedes birds.
Perhaps because he's such a lord of life

men, whose custom is to choose Barrabas,
torture him with such atrocities
as saintly Baudelaire has described in yon
sonnet built to cock a snook at time;
and Muse-loved Coleridge in his Mariner
made one such outrage universal drama –
the albatross as Barrabas' opposite number
and mankind with the Corpse around its neck,
achieving redemption only through love of Nature: –

> O happy living things! no tongue
> Their beauty might declare:
> A spring of love gush'd from my heart
> And I bless'd them unaware.

So is man's redemption only won
by finding once again his place in Nature,
loving as himself his neighbour creatures,
his Mother Earth, his genitor the Sun.

Lesser forms are no less albatross,
no less masters of the art of flight,
a dozen or so in all – the Laysan,
royal, short-tailed, yellow-nosed, the black-browed
albatross (one of which we had
recently on the Bass Rock here on Forth),
the waved albatross of the Galapagos:
not condors, eagles, nor any other birds
can equal them as champions of flight.

(32)

Milton, that grand organist of verse,
describes how Satan 'sat like a cormorant',
thereby upgrading him, degrading the bird
which never yet did aught was not ordained
by God through Nature, poor 'bald-headed raven',
as classifiers dub this name-luckless bird
who suffers much, as poets do, from slander
and all the ills defamed flesh is heir to.
No seven deadly virtues, no, nor sins,
at his feet can be laid by lying men,
though it is true they 'steal' from fishers' nets:
but who gave men proprietorial rights
in God's free gifts to all his earthly children?
The cormorants to men owe not one sou
though men derive tremendous wealth from them –
not only the fishing cormorants of the East
who dive for fish to bring up to their masters
but the guano cormorants enrich Peru
(and other of the South American countries),
and the Cape ones that South Africans exploit.
Of all wild birds most valuable to men.

First cousins to the snakebirds, cormorants
and shags, all thirty to forty species of the genus,
live no life of luxury at sea,
although they sun themselves with praying wings
(whether our Lord is visible or not)
but strenuous flying in pursuit of fish
in an element much weightier than air.
No flying aces like the albatross,
these great rump-footed birds lumber in air
bearing their bulk laboriously over
the reaching wave-tops – some can't fly at all
(the Harris cormorant, the Galapagos)
waddling along, just like a flippered penguin.

One half body and one half neck, the darters
can submerge like submarines (or grebes),
changing buoyancy at will in seconds,

spearing their prey the way skin-divers do
or (these snakebirds) as the cobra strikes,
triggering off at speed their z-bent neck.
The hunter's ways are many, though the end's the same,
and all four darters (species or variations?)
New World anhinga, Australian, Indian, African,
eat smaller, but no less well, than cormorants,
gobbling snakes, young alligators and newts.

Is it not strange the pelican should be
another amblem of Yeshua the Fish?
But legend says the pelican sheds its blood
(as he did) to feed its young in famine,
though legend tells us not which of the nine
species of the pelicans now known
was able so to sacrifice itself
(most likely a misunderstanding of
the young feeding on fish in the parents' gullet).
Ten-foot wing-span carries white pelicans
of Central America five score miles for food,
and some species soar like eagle or vulture,
while the brown, like the gannets, plunges for fish
stunning them often by sheer impact on water.
All five white species hunt in line like beaters
beating grouse, driving fish before them
into the shallows, to plunge on them together.

Sula bassana, the Bass Rock solan goose
can dive much deeper than any pelican,
open-winged plunging sometimes a hundred feet
to swallow a fish underwater, fly to the surface
and into the air again (like all nine gannets
including those the sailors miscall boobies).
Often round the Bass I've sailed in summer
marvelling at these mighty paper darts
dive-bombing the waves, or overhead
sailing and wheeling about the cry-scarred sky,
the cliffs white with them (and kittiwakes)
the yellow heads in evidence lower down,
the ice-grey eyes and sculptured dagger-beaks;
or watched them from Tantallon's ruined walls

as Gawin Douglas, Bishop of Dunkeld
and archbishop of poetry's vaster see
(our Scots language's greatest ever master,
Calliope's darling, jilted by Fortuna)
must have seen them five hundred years ago
plummeting down in the tormented waves:
or as I saw them first when, just a boy
in D'Arcy's entourage nearing May Isle,
one or two strayed over from the Bass
to wheel and dive near our lumbering boat.
Yet boobies too in some ways sure they are,
for every year the death-toll of their young
flightless left to feed on their own fat,
floating about untended on the swell
till their wings are strong enough to fly and dive,
is a stupid and appalling waste of life.
I myself once found a speckled youngster
on Portobello beach in Edinburgh,
helplessly blown from the Bass by an autumn storm
and, still unable to fly, starving to death.
So much for 'instinct', 'survival of the fittest'.

Where the not-so-remote Bermudas ride,
the gannet's kin, yon white-tailed tropic-bird
like some long-tailed, satin-finished dove-gull,
treats its young with similar abandon:
all six species, fond of sun-loved islands,
are typically solan in their habits
diving upon their little fish and squids
like white bodies falling from the sky,
so the bird men call them after Phaeton
struck by Zeus from the Sun his father's car.

Pity the schoolboy, all of eleven years,
who says when the class is asked what a 'frigate' is
'a bird' (as well as a boat): though my teacher
was one went home that night and checked the facts
and next day told the class that I was right.
Fregatidae, the marvellous frigate birds,
in ways outwing even the albatross,
swift as falcon (though with seven-foot wing-span)

lightly straddling the tameless mustang wind,
suddenly stooping to snatch a prey from the waves,
cocking a snook at death each time they do so:
for once in the water the frigate cannot rise
and hir oilless feathers drench and drag hir down.
But in hir element the air, hir speed
outflies all others, and like a giant skua
pirates boobies, cormorants, pelicans, gulls,
catching in air the prey they're forced to vomit.
Nesting among low trees on island rocks,
this gallant puffs his great red throat-pouch out
and burbles his raucous challenge to the air,
absurdly blustering, smaller than his mate,
as if to make up for his seeming lack of stature,
a black and red bird of incarnate pride –
the favourite sin of almost all male birds
but (as Blake said of the peacock's), the glory of God.
Five such glories have been vouchsafed Earth –
the great frigate bird, the magnificent,
the Ascension, the lesser, and the Christmas Island;
each a terrible Attila of the air,
a scourge of God upon its feathered kin.

(33)

Dylan writes of the heron-priested shore
and his sensation-seekers suitably amaze:
but the heron is no priest to sober eyes
as, like some litter-picker, it stilps about
the sea-weed backs of skerries at low tide
(as often I have seen it in St. Andrews)
or stands grey and silent in the burn
like old grey rags hung among the reeds,
its cold eye and old-age pensioner look
(straggles of grey hair sticking out behind)
seemingly as vacant as the sky
till some frog stirs or an eel or trout drifts near
and the javelin beak on the S neck leaps into life:
or weary as Methuselah near his end
heavily flaps towards the patient woods
where the raucous heronry outcaws the rooks
and makes the trees a dirty aerial slum.
And those night herons take advantage of
Edinburgh zoo's facilities.
Roosting and nesting there of their free will,
flapping about the duck and sea-bird ponds
helping the wing-cropped inmates eat their fish
(pelicans, gannets, shags, gulls and storks)
unmolested, not unwelcome guests:
in their great homeland in the Danube swamps
they breed in colonies with bitterns, egrets,
other heron, spoonbills and the like,
their tartar chicks tearing each other to bits
like any pack of academic critics.
Yet they survive with three-score other species
(most of them with their home-grown powder-puffs)
the various bitterns booming in the rushes –
most primitive, they say, of all the tribe.
Hudson watched one sway in time with the wind
sure in mind the shy one was more rushes.
That glorious snowy egret and her kin
(as Campbell saw them when the African night
sprayed her egrets on the still lagoons)
was almost done to death by vicious women.

The tiger-herons fish the shores of extinction
like so many kinds of daylight herons
(thirty-six or so that bird men tell of)
the pond and cattle herons, greens and blues,
purples, chestnut-bellied, squacco, Goliath
and imperials, Louisianas,
the African reef, the reddish egret, the greats,
the lessers, littles and leasts of Madagascar –
such plumeries of feathered skeletons!

Then their eccentric cousins, the Nile shoebills
(birds that seem half heron and half stork)
the boatbills of Brazil, grotesquely accoutred
as wierd survivors from the Reptile Age,
walking fossils outrageously alive.
The Life-artist, prodigiously prolific,
pours out hir living works in such profusion
as makes man's greatest geniuses look dry –
a living language makes the whole of English
seem but a basic, a pidgin dialect.

Another bird half heron and half stork,
the hammerhead of Africa, Madagascar,
a crow-black creature suited to the night,
proves categories are for men, not Nature
which cannot be reduced to mere abstractions,
builds a huge and three-roomed, covered nest
entered by a hole it has to squeeze through.
But hammerheads lead over to the storks,
jabirus and the fifteen other species
(all without the herons' powder-downs)
who, voiceless, can but clatter with their bills.
'Pelargos' in Greek, 'ciconia' in Latin,
but, in the Teutonic, just plain 'stork'.
Yet all of Europe loves the white stork
with almost superstitious reverence,
tallying their comings and their goings,
even providing platforms for the nesting
of this gannet-on-stilts of such good omen,
deeming lucky the rooftrees that they build on,
welcoming back from African wintering

often the same faithful pair as last year
returning to the same house and nest.
Few creatures are so honoured for their presence,
and few storks so honoured as the white:
the black, for instance, shuns the haunts of people,
loving the solitudes of swamp and forest,
though his cousin, the white-bellied, is
treated with respect in the Sudan
where it colonises trees in villages.
The black-necked stork of Asia and Australia,
the woolly-necked stork of Africa,
seem to encounter no such pampering,
nor the big saddle-bill (of African rivers)
with red and black beak and legs, much less
the giant marabouts which strut like colonels
among the other-rank vultures at kill or carrion
and so have earned the name of 'adjutants'.
But it's no officers' mess they rear their young in.
Hudson tells us the Maguari stork
of South America bounds like a kangaroo
along the ground before it gets airborne
above the pampas, river-bank or field
where it was preying on rodents, toads and reptiles.
And the jabirus, largest of New World storks,
lurk about prairie fires to feed upon
the wretched creatures fleeing from the flames.
Open-bills, whose beaks don't shut in the middle,
feed on mussels they set in the sun to gape
and other molluscs, fish and insect life.
The painted stork and the wood-ibises
(so-called) seem to be a link between
the stork clan and all true ibises,
wholly neither the one nor yet the other.

(34)

The sacred ibis of the Upper Nile
once worshipped in the Egypt of the Pharaohs
as the bird of Thoth, Osiris' secretary
(from whence derives, they say, Thoth-mas, my name)
no longer lives in that resurgent land,
has laid aside the heavy cares of state
which gave him then that bowed and solemn look
of bearing grave responsibilities,
as thoughtfully he treads the water edges.
But many other species are as solemn
(though none is secretary to a god) –
the beautiful scarlet ibis of Brazil
and Venezuela, the white of Mexico
(no Quetzalcoatl's amanuensis),
the glossy ibises of North America
(one of them is seen at times in Britain)
the African hagedash, the Indian black,
and others of this gravely stepping breed:
together with their spoonbill cousins, all
in all some twenty-eight varieties of them.
The roseate spoonbill of America
with carmine wings eclipses all four
Old World species, with their dominant white
(though slightly smaller than the European,
the African among his marshy reeds,
or the night-hunting Asiatic form).
Yet beautiful they stride forth, one and all,
scything the surface with their spatulas
to filter small crustaceans from the water.

But which of these long-legged, stilting chaps
associated under the sign of stork
compares with that rosy dream, the great flamingo?
The phoenix-winged, the classifiers call him,
phoenico-pteros, the bird goes down in flames
(as the Sun himself burns down in the west)
in countless club-beaked thousands – say upon
Tanganyika, Chad, Victoria Nyanza
or many another central African lake

where faint flamingoes burn among the reeds
(as Campbell, Scots-African bard has put it).
And in the towering Andes' rarified air
the largest of the four breeds haunts the lakes
where Indians, lama-capped, brave out the cold
as did their outraged (Inca and other) forebears
before the barbarous dagoes, mad for gold,
fouled all mankind with such atrocious crimes
as might have made the Sun itself turn pale
at sight of such inhuman degradation.
But these phoenix-wings of the Andes, white
birds with flaming scarlet wing-coverts,
look like going the way of Andean cultures,
steadily alas becoming rarer.
Here in Europe, still the rosy flamingo
and the lesser, thrive in Provence and Spain.
I myself (like seeing a pterodactyl)
have followed one in a car, one spring Sunday,
flapping improbably, long legs trailing,
from Seton sands almost to Prestonpans.
Elegant birds, so delicate and fragile,
they seem to be akin to storks and herons
but are in fact a kind of swan on stilts,
a link between the stork tribe and the geese,
like other links from tribe to tribe we've noticed.

(35)

What have geese in common with flamingoes?
A fatuous question, but the answer is a screamer
which, though outwardly it looks like neither,
inwardly is structured like them both –
this swan-sized bird of Amazonian swamps.
The one bird ribbed like the archaeopteryx,
without the chest-strengthening projections
all birds have (and even many reptiles),
and with air bubbles underneath the skin
which pop on pressure (unknown unless in gannets),
and ferocious spurs mounted on its wing-bends.
The three species pair, like swans, for life
it seems, their eggs too like swans', their young
swim like them, as heavily rise from water;
yet are chiefly waders, with great webless feet
and beaks more like pheasant than stork or goose –
a living Chinese puzzle of a bird
with a voice to frighten ghosts back into bodies.
Strangest of all, the bird men in their wisdom
clap on it the name of Palamedes
(*palus,* a swamp, has no doubt some part in it)
whom treacherous Ulysses framed and murdered
(which Homer's propaganda fails to tell us).
Thus, you see, ill-used by man and Nature
the horned screamer, the black-necked, and the crested,
scream because they've plenty to scream about.

I think that I shall never see a poem
lovely as a swan (to borrow Kilmer's
innocent lines of natural religion):
and that melodic honey old Saint-Saens
who helped Pavlova swan it on the stage,
also struck a true religious line.
But look, look how effortlessly there
that mute swan outswans the ballerina
in music no composer can achieve,
nor even the Swan of Avon can surpass
its poetry that outpoetries his verse,
the word incarnate on its Author's breath.

Yet (no mere word incarnate) he's a brute
as Yeats so truly saw him raping Leda:
look there, how his glide speeds up, his neck
S-bending for a strike as he lunges at
that harmless mallard; and when it squatters off
to land some yards away, brutally beats
the water with his wings to lumber after;
and how this village tyrant bullies, harries
the same wretched duck for no reason
but deviltry and brute intolerance.
And if this gentle-seeming poet-bird,
reflecting on the waters of the mind
and rummaging in them deep to sift his food
(brooding calmly on his own white image)
is violent and cruel, bloody-minded,
what shall we say of the awesome harpy eagle
crushing coney in its mighty talons?
True beauty contains a streak of terror
and the beauty of life is terrible indeed:
Edwin Muir I mind was shocked when I
pointed out this side of his holy Nature,
though nothing is to me more obvious,
nor troubles and distresses me so much.

Poets of course have always loved the swan
as emblem of themselves, in contempt of reason –
a mute bird for men with the gift of the gab!
Yeats saw it as the Romantic Age
drifting out upon the darkening flood,
and (little known among the honoured dead)
MacCaig makes it a swan-storm of itself;
and one of my favourite lines in my own work's
'Ang owre the tarn's mirk water smools the swan'
(a study, you may say, in black and white).
But one may linger far too long among
such beautiful and restful images:
it's time to note that all our swans are geese
(*anseres,* the classifiers tell us) –
and even our ducks (*anatidae*) O Hans!
The mute, the Bewicks, trumpeter or whooper,
Australia's red-billed black, the black-necked white

(discovered first in the Magellan Straits),
and smallest and most gooselike of them all,
the coscoroba – all with geese and ducks
are classified by the anatomists.
Would Pavlova have danced the Dying Goose?
But here we ride this poem's twin horses
the steed of poetry and the nag of science
together yoked in a poetry of fact
which I call 'polysemous veritism'
(from Dante's 'polysemous allegory').
These long-keeled and long-windpiped birds
who fly fast (though heavy), neck extended,
mostly sifting food as whales do krill,
though some (no swans) dive for fish and such;
all line nests with down from their own breasts;
and all their young fend quickly for themselves.

So all our geese and ducks are also swans:
the grey-lag goose, that sturdy vagabond
(so ruthless in his gluttony for bread
he picks one's pockets here at Duddingston Loch)
the barnacle, the brent, the Canada,
pinkfoot, white-browed (*albifrons*), the snow,
the bean, at times even the red-breasted,
all if only as migrants known in Britain:
the Australian semi-palmated, Cape Barren,
the kelp-goose of the Antarctic, the Chinese goose
(biggest of all) at home in eastern Asia
but kept in British ponds with our domestic
(the Egyptian) goose; some fourteen species in all
including the rare Hawaiian goose or nênē,
with eight species of tree or whistling ducks,
and the seven tribes of true anatidae
(the sheldrakes, river ducks, pochards, perching ducks,
sea ducks, the stiff-tailed, and the torrent) –
more species than I'll enumerate,
are all sib with the royal tribe of swans.

Mainly boat-shaped birds with paddle-feet
and prows like war-canoes, these navies make
another life-form straddle land and sea,

confident birds of aggressive burly ego
answering 'both, and', not 'either or';
determined to make the best of possible worlds.
These busty, pushing fellows, whether they be
near flightless penguins (like the steamer ducks),
swift as the mallard, teal, wigeon, or other
river ducks, pied like the sheldrakes, pochards,
golden-eyes, multi-coloured as mandarins,
perchers like the wattled Muscovy duck,
sea-going swimmers like eider, scaup or scoter,
omnivorous as the swan or (like mergansers
and goosanders) fixated on fishy diet;
soft-tailed as the tufted or stiff as Australia's
smelly musk duck; partial to quiet ponds
or bullering streams (like the Andes torrent duck) –
all seem to wear success like a uniform.
Land, sea and air they can make free of
without machines. Our notocord has come
a long way from the lancelets and the lampreys.

(36)

What could be less like a heron or a stork
then the falcon hatchet-man who strikes it down?
Yet they are close akin, the bird men tell us,
while owls are not at all like hawks but swifts:
the world of seeming's not the world of is.
And after ducks the next link in the chain
of being's not, as you'd think, the great sea eagle
but a bird as far from it as you'd imagine –
the heaviest flying bird, the Andes condor
and other vultures of the Americas.
The giant condor equals the albatross
in span of wing, though bulkier in frame:
yet he's no eagle, power-clawed for prey,
but a feeble-footed carrion scavenger
(food so foul would poison any eagle).

Certain Pueblo of the upper Andes
see his mighty wings as the power of spirit,
and in their festivals lash a condor's feet
to a wild horse, to symbolise the struggle
between the pinioned spirit and the flesh,
(a struggle as perverse as it is cruel
for the spirit *is* the flesh, the flesh the spirit),
rejoicing if their Mazeppa bird survives
the ordeal of its ride with wings unbroken.
Its fellow condor of California
hovers, as I write, on the edge of extinction
(less than sixty orange heads now counted):
and once departed may return no more.

Others of these New World vultures (cathars,
so the bird men call them, purifiers)
are less threatened, certainly less in size:
the king-vulture, white eye set in vermilion,
turkey-vulture and its twin, the black
(both widespread and both nesting aground,
scavengers of village and small town),
the Californian vulture, threatened by cattlemen,
and Central America's yellow-headed vulture,

(all with a hole bored through the beak for nostrils,
no medial bone like the Old World vultures):
some of them no bigger than big hawks.
All such birds have sight highly developed
and when one towering bird dives down to food
another notes it and follows down, another
sees that, and soon, as by bush telegraph
or chain-reaction, birds from miles around
are gathered for what pickings may be going.

A long-tailed eagle set on a crane's legs
with quill pens stuck behind both ears,
the secretary-bird, that Attila
of snakes, that Minister of Snake Control,
links the New World vultures with the Old.
Four feet tall from the time they leave the nest
(an untidy pile of sticks on a thorn-tree top)
they pounce on even cobras with their feet,
parrying the strikes with hurtless wings
until they can seize the head and batter it on
some rock, the ground, or if the snake's too big,
lug it up in the air and let it fall.
But they also feed on vermin and young birds
and hug the cruel edges of prairie fires
to snatch creatures lucky enough to flee them.
Eagle-eyed, alert, precise and swift,
to me they call up T. S. Eliot,
that minister of (if not the gods) the Muses
and scourge of many literary snakes.

I should have said 'a vulture on crane's legs'
for the bird men say the secretary-bird
is kin of Old World Vultures, the lammergeier
or bearded vulture (a giant once of the Alps
but long since hunted thence to kindlier places
where it planes for hours above unclimbable cliffs);
the hooded vulture of East Africa
(which like many seems an offshoot from eagles),
the white Egyptian vulture (or neophron),
the griffon, his cousin the long-billed vulture,
the black, the Pondicherry and many another

such as I've seen gathered on tin roofs
above the meat-market in Kaduna,
or squabbling like whelps over offal on the ground:
raw-necked and repulsive, to my eye
nowise like the noble secretary.

Of all this tribe of souls, these vultures, eagles,
buzzards, kites, falcons, harriers, hawks
ospreys and caracaras, the students have
identified for science five hundred species,
a caste of ruthless proud aristocrats
ferocious as so many feudal barons.
The eagles are the kings, the bateleurs
of Africa (with crimson face and legs
among the most striking), our golden eagle,
the white-tailed, magnificent sea-erne,
the serpent-eagle, the Philippine monkey-eagles
and, most awe-inspiring, the harpy eagle
(lobo volante, Mexico's flying-wolf)
that preys on fawns, monkeys, lambs and foxes,
its awesome head (with great round ruff and ears)
that of some medieval executioner
(or harpy mask from Greek tragedy)
and great claws could throttle a man to death;
the bird-nest eagle of Indonesian parts
that harries nests of all their eggs or young,
the crowned-eagle of the African tropics,
the great bald sea-eagle (the U.S. emblem),
ferocious-beaked Pacific (Steller) sea-eagle;
the booted, spotted, the Bonelli eagle,
haunt our human minds as no other birds,
favourite symbols of imperial power,
or spiritual, or intellectual.
Yet the poets have preferred the singing-birds,
the nightingales, the larks, the bulbuls and thrushes,
peaceful birds compared with these predators –
though Hopkins saw a kestrel as his Christ.

Easily I could sing the eagle's might
aloft on his towering wings on mountain wastes
where Zeus used him to torture mankind's friend;

or even among our homelier Scottish bens.
But I have heard this proud conqueror mew
like a kitten, and caught the pathos in that voice
(just as, out at sea, I've sympathised
with the terrible pathos of the fulmar's cry).
To me he is no Attila of the air
to awe the heart, but a fellow-sufferer
born to endure his pain as I do mine;
no heraldic emblem, but a living soul
caught on the wheel of living, just like us,
hatched, matched and despatched, will he nill he,
like us a creature of an unknown Creator,
a Mystery beyond our comprehension
(though often called the Life-force, God, reality),
never less understood than when most expressed.

Kin of the sea-eagle, the lizard-eating
gymnogenes (and other harriers)
nest upon the ground like any game-bird
(the marsh, the hen, the Montagu's harrier
and fourteen other species known to us)
haunters of swamps for frogs, lizards and such,
large, light, long-legged and elegant birds
mostly with facial discs like those of owls;
like owls too they hunt in the night or twilights,
prowling low above the reeds and rushes –
the males, as usual, smaller than their mates.

The buzzards too are of this eagle clan
and only size at times distinguishes
the lesser from the greater bird (I've noticed)
as the buzzard wheels and soars above the bens.
But the buzzard among hawks is best included
(as in the States) ninety species or so,
and the honey buzzard breaking open hives
really is much nearer to the kites.
Best known of the hawks to poem and story
(though not to sight), the medieval goshawk,
terror of the herons, our humorous bird men
name 'gentilis', just as its feudal masters
(gang of greedy gleds) were called the gentry –

'gentle' traitors sorning off the peasants.
The kestrel (no hawk really but a falcon)
we all have seen on set-square wings hover
over parks even in capital cities
as I have seen (from Edinburgh Castle)
them hover over Princes Street gardens,
or nesting undisturbed among the pigeons
on the rock itself, or Scott's monument.
And Hopkins, that Welsh English symphonist
(mouthing delicious syllables like his sloe
which, mouthed to flesh-burst, gushed, so flushed the man ...)
immortalised it in impetuous music
(though some of the poem sits ill at ease with truth).
The sparrow-hawk I've seen (though much less common)
fearlessly inspect me from a fence
up in Argyll beside the river Shiel
(and, rarely, still see hunt by wood or hedgerow):
but the lord of falcons in the British isles
is the homing-pigeon's foe, the peregrine,
a bird of quite incomparable beauty,
chieftain above all that clan includes:
the merlin's gun-metal wings and russet front,
the lanner's deep chestnut, the saker's light,
the Eleanore's brooding dark as storm-cloud,
the singing-hawks, the cuckoo-hawks or bazas,
the hobby (like a smaller peregrine) –
superb birds, but never gentilis!

That fork-tailed kite with his cold eye
somehow suits the wild tors of Wales,
though his black and black-winged cousins
rarely stray across from bedevilled Europe.
But here in Scotland every summer season
the royal ospreys visit on Loch Garten
(guarded like the important guests they are
against marauders twenty-four hours a day)
noble birds who plunge hard down on fish,
lugging them in their talons from the spray
to feed on the flesh in some tree's branches.

The caracaras of the Americas

often feed on carrion, among vultures.
The crested, and red-throated caracara
(among the other species of the clan)
were thought akin to secretary-birds:
but anatomists ally them with the falcons.
Like secretary-birds they too eat snakes,
amphibians and lizards, as well as carrion:
a curious and many-sided race
allied to vultures and to falcons both,
to secretary-birds and falconets.

(37)

So far in bird form much has been achieved:
great range in use of four-limbed skeleton
with forelegs feathered wings for pursuit and flight;
the egg that gives each chick its own bit ocean
to start life in (as all such beings must)
in a womb of shell laid outside the mother;
the myriad variations played by species.

Yet each achievement's hedged by limitations:
still must parent body heat the eggs
in sacrifice of freedom, food and safety;
still must chicks be parent-fed for weeks
till strong enough to forage for themselves.
Could parents not be freed from brooding duties?
Could not the chicks from hatching feed themselves?
Such things are commonplace among the reptiles
(and birds are lizards turned their scales to feathers).
Are there no birds have tried to solve the problem,
freed themselves from such a tyrannous thralldom?
Certain game-birds win their liberation.

There are those birds Australians call brush-turkeys,
the megapodes (or muckle-feet) to science,
though far enough in kind from turkeys proper.
These birds with their gigantic, strong-toed feet
kick up the soil and dead leaves into mounds
of twenty to a hundred feet all round,
or even more as they build up through years.
At depths of two-three feet huge eggs are laid
(big enough to fully fledge the chicks)
and left for the Sun and heat of decay to hatch;
so when at last these full-fledged chicks break out
they scramble through the mould to begin at once
to forage for themselves like adult birds –
in some species chicks can even fly.
The parent simply checks the temperature
from time to time, making needed adjustments,
like any cook with casserole in the oven:
but the half-dozen eggs are sixty-three days cooking.

Necessity has mothered this invention,
for these scrubland birds must forage miles each day
to stay alive; brooding would mean starvation.

Variously called thermometre-birds,
mound-builders, mallee fowl (or scrub fowl),
incubator-birds, or brush-turkeys,
they eat berries, insects, crabs and snails.
Some kinds inhabit Malaya, Micronesia,
and New Guinea, supplanting there the pheasants
(which lack the adaptation to such living).
These birds have been a benefit to man
in divers ways; their mounds serve as islands
in flooded scrub or jungle; the birds themselves
saved soldiers from starvation in the War
(eaten, on some islands, to extinction);
and from immemorial times the abo bushmen
have farmed the eggs (but rarely eat a bird),
the mounds, as property, to families allotted.

Different species vary in form and methods
from pigeon-size to turkey, from the compost mound
to the habit of using (like the Celebes maleo)
hot black sand, or the earth around hot springs,
to do their incubating. They swarm down
from the mountains to the black, sandy shores
in breeding season (the full-fledged chicks somehow
making their way alone back up the mountains);
or near hot springs, high up in the hills,
dig burrows in the volcanic soil
and leave their eggs to incubate in its heat.

(38)

These so-called 'game' birds (no 'game' to them,
be sure), birds like our own barnyard fowl
descended from the Burmese jungle cock)
are all ground scrabbling, mainly for seeds
and such, yet mostly roosting in tree or bush,
mostly capable only of short, swift flight.
They all have crops to pre-digest hard grain,
all have filo-plumes below the feathers
(the chicks self-feeding from the time of hatching),
and most of them have spurs upon the legs.
South American curassows are such,
guans, penelopes and chachalacas
(close related to the muckle-feet
but wanting their great inventive genius)
building nests of sticks like other birds
in trees or on the ground, and brooding there.
Thirty-eight species or so there are in all,
cousins of turkeys, pheasants, grouse and quail,
ranging in size from the little chachalaca
(wheepling at forest edges) to the great curassow
big as turkey, black and white and crested,
the cock with great yellow pobble on his brow;
the razor-billed curassow and the crested;
the black penelope; the horned guan
and the wattled; the helmeted curassow;
the sickle-winged guan; the Gray's curassow –
a plentiful crew, crowding out the jungles,
sometimes kept as free-range pets by natives
(begging tit-bits from the family,
following the children on their errands).

But the game birds proper, as the bird men say
(and some would say the ones that bring in money)
are wider spread and far wider known:
the turkeys, pheasants, partridges, grouse and quail,
most important of all, the jungle fowl
from which our lucrative chickens are descended;
the prim-headed guinea-fowls of Africa
where I have seen them wild in a lost valley

near Jos (Nigeria) breenge out from the cliff
uttering alarms like grouse or pheasant
and whirr, in spotty grey, across the ravine
where, far below, the black dots of bushmen
mattocked the ground a rainbow lay upon:
the wild American turkey, like our farm one
with hir brassy stare and red raw caruncles,
and hir ocellated cousin, wild and shy.
Best known of all, the great pavone,
the crested peacock whose pride is God's glory,
who needs at least his mirrored image to strut at
(lest he pine and die for want of audience),
his great tail-coverts with their peacock eyes,
the ornament of palaces and parks –
a bird in danger of sinking in its emblem.
How many have even heard of his rarer cousins,
the secretive ones of Burma and the Congo?

Mellower in tone, the argus pheasant
is little less resplendent than the peacock
when all its eye-spot feathers are outspread
like some great fan, in courtship displays
(proud indeed as Argus might have been
as ever poet's eye imagined him).
Sumatra and Siam and suchlike places
add these jewels to their other treasures
while Borneo and Tonkin can make boast
of the smaller Gray's and Rheinhardt's crested species
(this last the rarest game-bird of the clan).
The same Indo-Malay part of the world
have also peacock-pheasants (blend of riches)
sheltering (some) their broods with fanning tails,
their peacock-eyes dotting the outer feathers:
and most important for mankind of all
that red jungle-fowl surnamed Bankiva
(denizen of those deep and steaming jungles),
ancestor of our farmyard cocks and hens
(now a battery industry whose horror
only its necessity condones).

For me the glory of game-birds was and is

our local pheasant of russet-metal plumes
that glint and glow in light as fine's the peacock's:
not only the living bird on wing or foot
but the murdered one roasted for the table –
a taste acquired in boyhood when, unable
to pay the annual game licence fee,
I brought the occasional whirring pheasant down
when one exploded under my rabbiting gun,
obeying the Law, but breaking the laws of men
(till, caught and fined, I gave up the gun forever,
sold it, and bought myself a better fly rod).
These Chinese ring-necked pheasants we have here
have long ousted an earlier (native?) breed:
but other aliens failed to naturalise.
Just think if in our woods and fields we saw
not one but the scores of species in the world:
the gorgous golden pheasant (also from China)
the Amherst (with its dark metallic greens),
the barred-back, silver, fire-backed, and white-crested,
mikado, great-eared, and the Bulwer's wattled,
the Himalayan tragopans and moonals,
the ocellated pheasant of Indo-China –
not just in our zoos but free and ranging
(or at least as much so as our common ring-neck),
living ornaments, at large and breeding!

And those minor pheasants I sometimes also shot,
the partridges that creak about in coveys –
think if to the common species here
we added some of the rich varieties,
the red-legged, rock, and Barbary partridges
(really were quite common here I mean),
the snow, the tooth-billed, the scaly and the plumed,
the thick-billed partridge of Amazonia,
Africa's forty-four kinds francolins,
the seven breeds of quail, the wood partridge –
as sensible to sigh for paradise.
Even if such birds adopted us,
the paradise would only attract more guns.

And what of eighteen species of the grouse,

the feather-footed ones, the lagopods?
The red grouse is our own Scottish bird
(and for that reason surnamed Scoticus)
a bird that seems the spirit of the heather
incarnated in this avian form,
a complex bird of many colour-changes
(climatic more than seasonal in nature)
living, nesting close to mother Earth
and shouting hir defensive cry 'go back!'
whenever foot intrudes upon hir empire.
But others of the clan have an especial
kinship with the Scots and our tough land –
the black cock (and grey hen) whose lyral tail
is stuck in regimental (and other) bonnets
(though this black grouse is found in other airts)
is almost as native Scottish as the red;
and in these isles at least the capercailyie
(mighty bruiser of the North's pine forests)
is as native Scottish as the Grampians
where he bellows his excited love-spel out
(absorbed in it as Lehmann was in lieder)
tail fanned out like some red Indian head-dress.
Ptarmigan too somehow seem native Scots,
white-feathered for the snow like willow-grouse
in vain attempt to hide from enemies:
some of the four species live only abroad –
the white-tailed one of Americanada,
the rock species of Europe and Eurasia,
and the willow one of the New and Old World arctic.
Grouse of course have also many species
no more Scottish than a Samoyed:
the ruffled grouse, and the spruce of Canada,
mainstay of many an oldtime pioneer;
the blue or dusky grouse of the Rocky Mountains,
and other kinds to the New World peculiar –
prairie chicken, sage hen, sharp-tailed grouse
in several varieties, for instance,
and the hazel hen of Europe and central Asia
we're never like to find in the Lammermuirs.

(39)

All these birds devoted to the land!
But water is the largest part of Earth
and still must claim the lion share of life:
so cranes that demoiselle about the marshes
and rails that chicken in the shallow waters
are two of many kinds that compromise
between the life on land and that on ocean,
so much preferring water and ground to air
that flight is weakened or (in some) quite lost.
Shawling Tristan da Cunha's flightless rail;
mesites, roatelos and Bensch's monias
(those rare birds of rare-rich Madagascar)
all with wings they never put to use,
preferring to trust their legs and camouflage.
Strange birds that baffle the classifiers:
the black-spotted russet and white mesite
with legs and other characters like rails
but powder-downs like herons or like cranes
(St. Hilaire aligns them with the pigeons
instead of with the seemingly nearer kiwis);
the reddish brown mesite or roatelo;
the grey male monia, his brick-red hen
(neither bigger than a missel-thrush,
the males mostly bringing up the young).
Even Madagascar has few birds weirder.

But of the six or seven scores of species
unarguably classified as rails
our common corncraik (getting not so common)
unseen creaking among the ungathered harvest
(like Ruth among the not so alien corn)
together with the coot and water-hen
(the meer-fowl) for us are typical.
Sombre-coloured (mostly) birds, and squat
with hennish legs and often lengthy toes,
secretive, silent, modest little birds
creeping through grain-stalks, forests, reedy marshes
or bobbing and ticking over ponds and rivers,
able to fly, but much preferring not to,

and if compelled, only for meagre distance.
Yet some migrate and actually hit skyscrapers,
meeting a nightmare end in the streets of cities.
Others, like the Tristan rail and that of Guam,
Wake, and other Pacific isles, are flightless,
having for far too long no enemies
to keep them airborne: and some have succumbed
dodo-like, to domestic predators.
Such diving rails as water-hens and coots
will surely (like the ducks) in time evolve
webbed feet? The coot already has
the lobed (half-webbed) toes of all the grebes –
our common coot, the giant one of Peru,
the American, the Bonaparte's horned
coot of Bolivia that builds its nest
of pebbles high above the Andes snowline
(for want of vegetation lined with algae);
the knob-billed coot of parts of Africa,
and many another species of the genus;
and those great water-hens, the gallinules
in royal purple O so perjinckly stepping
with great shielded beaks and crimson legs.

New Zealand, that front-porch of paradise
for those of us who hunt the noble trout,
seems for ground birds too a paradise
(or was till men brought dangerous enemies).
Yet the kiwi holds its own, and of the rails
the tawny weka rail still survives
big as a hen, hunting rats and mice
(though almost hunted to death, once for its oil);
the takahe too (once pronounced extinct)
flightless like the weka, clings to life
among the other rails on Maui's Fish.
Hawaii and Laysan have flightless rails;
America its sora rail, its clapper,
ypecaha wood-rail, the five-inch black rail;
and Africa its black crake, among others –
a highly successful species, you may say,
exploring what the soul-thing can create
in avian form, from the ground and inland waters.

Halfway from rails to cranes, or so it seems,
the long-beaked courlans hold their niche
in swamps and rivers, eating mainly molluscs:
the limpkin of the Florida everglades
(a purply-chocolate bird flecked with white)
and the inconsolably-wailing lamenting bird
(or crazy widow) of Amazonia:
and the three kinds of their cousin trumpeters
from similar terrain, tamed by Brazilians
and set to guard their other domestic fowl
(as geese once saved the Romans from us Celts),
their ventriloquial voice a siren-system.

(40)

And you my lovelies, you high-stepping cranes,
your very name a gently plangent poem,
often diameded, crowned like bygone ladies,
as much like storks as princesses like women
O petite-nosed artistocrats of birds
superbly gowned in feathered elegance!
Mainly north-east Asian birds, they go
south for winter, and nest on reedy mounds
after a courtship mimics ball-room dancers.
The common crane (what crane was ever 'common'!)
known in England in pre-Labour times
grey as a winter day; the whooping crane
of Mexico and north America;
the beautiful Japanese white with grey-black throat;
the even whiter Asiatic white;
the crowned crane of Mallorca and Africa;
the black-necked crane, the sandhill crane,
Australia's brolga, the brave Siberian,
the semi-sacred sarus of the paddies –
how long will all their kind be spared to us?
You above all, my diva, demoiselle,
deigning at times to slum with us in Europe,
petite Charmaine, delighting our eyes and ears,
us brute men to your shy, delicate beauty!
I spread my poem for you to walk on, lady.

In South America the cariamas,
little Burmeister's and the crested one,
superficially like the secretaries,
nevertheless are anatomical cranes
(descended from the fossil phororhacos)
haunting the pampas, woodlands and savannahs
(the cresteds nest aground, Burmeister's in trees)
feeding on snails and insects, worms and snakes
(for which their brother humans guard and tame them).
And in New Caledonia the kagu
sports its powder-downs like crane or heron
but (unlike them) all its body over:
a bird with large erectile crest, much given

to wing-display, but tottering on extinction,
a bird of the night (a night soon to be endless)
harried by man and his domestic beasts,
with only one-chick broods to make good losses –
beautiful red-legged tumblers, worth conserving.
So too hir cousins, the so-called sun-bitterns,
birds of Brazil's and Guatemala's forests
given, wise birds, to worship of our Star
(source of all earthly life and earthly goodness)
gold-red wings to His rays raised from the water,
surely one of Nature's most deserving.

And, strangest of all, the so-called sun-grebes
or (even worse-called) finfeet, wretched birds
by the naming Muse so slightingly disfavoured
(except for their official 'heliornis'),
they too are cranes, all three, though more like grebes
in superficial shape, with lobed feet
(not webbed or finned) with grebe-like bills and nostrils:
fresh-water birds of only the warmer climates
(the Far East, Africa, South America)
where they prey on fish and other water creatures.

(41)

Where ends the crane? Why, where the plover begins.
But where begins the plover? Where ends the crane!
Another way of saying that silly questions
evoke silly answers, for Nature seldom
accommodates the classifying mind.
Life delights in breaking its own laws
to prove all law subservient to Life.
So these crane-like plovers, the jacanas,
rail-like also, often with pheasant tails
(therefore called water-pheasants), these lily-trotters
(walking on water-lilies in sluggish waters)
play hide-and-seek with schoolmarm classifiers,
their weight on the lily-leaves by long toes spread,
asserting the elusiveness of Nature.
In keeping with such flouting of conventions,
the sexes largely interchange their roles,
the little male mothering the young,
his big aggressive mate to him displaying
as males of normal birds to females do.
Seven kinds there are (at time of writing)
spread across a wide span of the world:
Texas to Argentina, Madagascar,
Africa, Java, India, Malaya,
Ceylon, Australia, Panama, New Guinea –
the comb-crested, the pheasant-tailed, the lesser,
the bronze-winged and other lily-trotters:
living demonstrations of adaptation.

Once upon a time (and long before
that nowhen date of so many fairy tales)
great bustards roamed on Salisbury Plain
and other parts of England (if not Scotland)
but now no longer roam – no fairy tale.
Cranes and plovers in part, wholly bustards
unique selves (like most pigeon-holed creatures)
defying the classifiers and extinction
(looking most like little ostriches)
I've seen them strut the African savannah
(or was it their greater cousin the gam-paaum?)

near Kaduna on the Nigerian plateau:
and in Germany and Russia still they're nesting,
thirty-pound weight, eight-foot wing-spanned birds
with curious side-whiskers and tails of turkeys.
Even to-day they stray across the channel,
as the little bustard does and the houbara:
but rarer than good summers here in Scotland.

Plovers proper, the birds who like the rain,
(pluvia) and mud, the mud-dwellers
(*limicolae* – inhabitants of mud),
those busking characters, clown of music-hall
complete with patter (the *charadridae*),
wild as the open moors and estuaries
where often I have seen these many kinds –
the ringed, the green, the grey, the golden plover
(the two last named like a flight of arrows
hurtling past my young wildfowling head
but leaving some of their flock to bless my table),
the lapwing (green) a constant country companion:
and the little ringed one fussing along the shores
and skerries of my briny-aired St. Andrews.
There too curlews burbled at low tide,
the oyster-catchers frisked the tangled rocks
and frightened the air with their alarmist cries
while sandpipers and redshanks busied about
and flipped along the crests of crowding rollers;
turnstones cased sometimes the littoral pebbles
and, rarely, godwits probed the ebbing fringes.
Knots and dunlins I'm not sure of seeing
nor the purple sandpiper yonder on the May;
dotterels no, nor greenshanks, whimbrels yes
come back to me from those green years long gone.
Others of the clan are more exotic:
New Zealand wrybills, avocets and stilts,
ibis-billed curlews, phalaropes,
the curlew sandpiper and the pectoral,
the (late Elizabethen) ruff and reeve
(which in display flaunt themselves into a trance),
dowitchers and various sanderlings.
But on the moors and marshes I had seen

common snipe and jack snipe twist and turn
and rarely (by some fir-wood) flushed a woodcock.
Pin-tailed snipe of course I never saw
nor the so-called 'painted snipes' (sandpipers really)
of South America, India, Africa, Australia.

Overseas with them, the spur-winged lapwing
picks the teeth (it's said) of crocodiles
in Egypt and in other likely haunts:
the masked plover of Australasia
able to kill or blind snakes and lizards
with the spurs it bears on the wrist-joints of the wings;
the red-wattled lapwing and the banded plover
spoil the sport of hunters near the paddies,
circling and screaming as if mobbing owls;
the killdeers in the north Americas
(lapwingless) fill the lapwings' niche;
and the New World (only) surf birds like the turnstones
dash about in the fringes of the breakers.
In some of these, the phalarope for instance,
the female woos the male who builds the nest,
hatches out the eggs and rears the chicks:
these 'cootfoot' females wear the gaudy feathers,
lording it over the plain and smaller males,
and in migration these sea plovers may
land and feed on the backs of whales and such,
or feed on the life they churn up in their wake.

The pratincoles ('inhabitants of meadows')
on Niger banks I've seen, but on meadows never,
wheeling about the sand or gravel banks
(*glareolidae* – the gravel-birds
as they and the coursers are in Latin named)
protruding from the river – swallows in flight
to look at as, swallow-like, they feed on the wing
(surely most unploverlike behaviour):
but see them like dunlins scamper over the gravel.
The long-legged coursers are more like true plovers
but slender of curlew bill; the isabelline
or cream-coloured courser touches Britain at times,
but one of them also is a crocodile bird

picking the leeches out of those terrible jaws:
and their distant kin, the crab-plover, scours
the seashores of Africa's east coastline,
a black-winged white bird with a heavy beak
for dealing with the shells it has to crack.

The South American seed-snipes are no snipes
(though their flight is snipelike) much less partridges
(though that is what they look like), stubborn eccentrics
and non-conformers, grouped somehow with the plovers.
From the Patagonian tundra and Falkland Isles
to the upper Andes of tropical Peru
they make the colder wastes their habitat,
feeding mainly on seeds and such-like fodder,
little knowing man (and better for it).
Stone curlews (or thickknees) also baffle
those who think that God can be pigeon-holed,
reality trapped in nets of words, the great
mystery of Being (beyond all knowing)
kept in musty drawers like the skins of birds
tagged or labelled, magicked by mere names.
Like Oedipus, yon tyrant king of Thebes,
they dub hir 'oedicnemus', but the bird
(like poets who're defamed by slanderous critics)
is always so much more than any name –
a bit like a bustard, yet grouped with plovers,
an insect eater in semi-deserts
(and certainly no curlew), the several species
will always (I hope) baffle the pin-downers,
asserting life against mere formulation.

But avocets, those delicate high-steppers,
queen this clan like some world mannequins,
match-sticks of miraculous assemblage
in a white gown slashed and caped with black,
rivalled by the daddy-longlegs stilts –
birds too frail, you'd say, for brute existence:
and men and rats indeed have brought some
at least of the species almost to extinction,
our own Old World avocet among them.

(42)

Half-way between the plovers and the gulls,
the beautiful white-sheath-bills hold a niche
in wintry desert isles in the antarctic
where man is little known and so little feared
that these two species (the white and lesser sheath-bill)
come up close to take a look at him.
Eaters of seaweed (and life found in seaweed),
their high infant mortality ensures
they'll never hunt the fulmars from our cliffs.

But the gulls themselves, those birds that Huxley showed
to be the plovers' anatomical kin
(a kinship shows too in their similar eggs),
a bold, omnivorous race throughout the world
whose eyes reflect a stoic view of life,
a Nature-vision far from sentimental.
And of this tribe the ancientest (it's said)
is by far the skua – the variety of skuas,
the vomit-eaters (*stercorariidae*)
who harry terns and other fishing gulls
to force them disgorge (that they may grab) their fish
(usually before they hit the water) –
unromantic Turpins of the air.
The mighty bonxie, known as great skua,
harries also nests (and young penguins
are a favourite food on breeding sites),
and I have seen them, with the larger gulls,
scour the Bass for chicks in breeding season
(even the lordly gannets not immune),
and from my windows here in Portobello
seen the arctic skua (America's jaeger)
harry the screaming terns along the shore –
great dark swallows loose from hell,
angels from the murky realms of Satan
routing, as it seemed, their opposite numbers.

Here on the Forth, among my daily familiars
the common, herring, and black-headed gulls,
the lesser, and at times the great, black-backed,

occasional kittiwakes among the fulmars
and, in summer months, the commoner terns,
carve their pains upon the cry-cut air.
And one November Sunday when the arctic
wind icicled to tears my eyes,
a great white gull at the mouth of the Figgate burn,
magnified by the tear-films on my eyes
almost to albatross size, a glaucous gull
like an outsize herring gull with no black tips,
seemed the incarnate spirit of his arctic home.
The commoner gulls here stand around all day
or idly sail about the empty sky
as if they were above such chores as feeding –
the opposite of the frantic oyster-catchers
ceaselessly probing the fringes of the waves
or other of the anxious ebb-tide feeders.
When do these scavengers do their scavenging?
And sometimes on a steamer, sailing to Skye,
or merely down the Clyde and round the Kyles,
I feed convoying gulls with bread from fingers,
amazed at how secure between their wings
they seem to sit, like granny in her rocker,
more at home on the wind than I aground.
Sometimes I tease them, holding onto a crust
to knock them off their equilibrium.
Like vultures, gulls at sea will hunt en masse,
the descent of one on food triggering off
a signal calls in gulls from all directions,
perfect masters of flight (in that like small
albatrosses), wings with zoa between –
some forty-three species of the clan.
Pacific gulls that decimate young turtles,
glaucous gulls drop crabs on rocks to crack them
(as lammergeiers crack bones for their marrow),
Buonaparte's gull that nests in evergreens,
the ivory gull that seldom leaves the arctic
like the black-collared, rosy Ross's gull;
the little gull and the ring-billed (smallest of all),
kittiwakes (who are the most oceanic,
wandering far out on the northern oceans),
the great black-headed, the slender-billed, the Iceland,

Audouin's, and the Mediterranean gull,
the Californian gull (saved Salt Lake City
in pioneering days from a plague of locusts),
Franklin's gull and Sabine's – O so many,
Nature dazes the mind with admiration,
with the Life-artist's overflowing genius!

Thaer him stearn oncwaeth, isigfethera ...
'riposted the ice-feathered tern', the Seafarer says
(though which of the forty species he doesn't tell),
but for me they're all associates of May,
not only of the month that brings them here
(to my ear welcome harbingers of summer)
but the Isle of May with D'Arcy in my boyhood,
terns in colonies so thick the foot
dared scarcely move for trampling eggs or chicks,
the air a screaming snowstorm of the birds
(common, arctic, Sandwich and little terns
with a few roseates high above the storm)
diving outraged at our intruding heads,
like angels on fiends gatecrashing paradise.

My heart leaps up (to parody WW)
when I behold sea-swallows in the sky,
birds whose cries are discords to their beauty:
the arctic tern who so adores the light
of day he moves from pole to pole
to live the year in nearly permanent day;
Forster's tern that haunts the Canadian tundra
in spring for chilled-alive fish as they unfreeze;
the Inca tern of the west of Andes coastline;
the sooty tern of Ascension (which ignores
seasons, breeding four times in a three-year stretch);
the pure white fairy terns of Pacific atolls
in tree-forks laying (nestless) one white egg;
gull-billed terns that sometimes feed on insects
(caught in the air while flying far inland);
little terns (presenting fish in courting);
white-winged black terns, Caspian, black, and whiskered,
the noddies who attack (even men) to kill –
Nature nothing if not prodigal,

spendthrift of her numberless life-treasures.

Lower bill longer than the upper, the skimmer
shears the water with its beak wide open
to snatch up fish or shrimp that bumps into it,
wings long and pointed for such gliding.
Their eyes uniquely geared for night and day,
night they prefer for prey's then more abundant,
and leave behind a phosphorescent wake
(whether on ocean or inland lakes or rivers)
which signals in more prey for their return.

(43)

Man, with his improvident destruction
of miracles beyond his greatest powers,
murdered (among others) the great auk
which paid the price (in flightlessness ashore)
for its underwater-diving adaptation.
Men had slain the lot by nineteen hundred.
But the razorbill, the great auk's lesser cousin,
still delights the visitor to islands
(as here around the Bass, the Lamb, the May)
where they breed and clamour on the sheerest cliff-face
outnumbered by their upright guillemot kin.
Both of them I've picked up on the seashore
dead or alive (oiled up or exhausted).
And that delightful auk, the stocky puffin,
our 'little arctic friar' with massive bill
of red, blue and yellow, snow-white cheeks
and vest, black coat and cap, with orange legs,
six fish at a time in beak for the chicks –
surely one of Nature's entertainers,
for most of us too difficult of access.
I remember D'Arcy's lab man once on the May
thrust his arm in a burrow up to the shoulder,
pulled out not the expected puffin but a rabbit.

Some twenty-two of the auk tribe still survive,
penguin-like, yet all with power of flight.
D'Arcy I remember commenting
on the steep angle razorbills can rise at
up the cliffs, as we approached May Isle,
amazed by what he called 'these dumpy birds'.
Storms at times can decimate some species
(guillemots and razorbills for instance)
not by their rage, but by forcing down the fish
to depths beyond the reach of diving birds
so that the poor wretches die of starvation.
Penguin-like, though not in fact related,
these second cousins of the gulls and terns
are to the north what penguins are to the south:
are they then, new penguins in the making?

Or will their nesting keep their flight alive?
These guillemots (Americans call them 'murnes')
including the black (American 'sea-pigeon')
the little auk (American 'dovekie')
which has, like the lemming, suicidal drives,
the marbled murrelet of the north Pacific,
the ancient murrelet, the crested auklet,
the least auklet, and the parroquet
together with their dandy puffin brother –
will they and the remainder of the auks
be in a million years so many penguins?

(44)

Columbidae, the clan of birds of peace,
of doves and pigeons and the so-called sand-grouse:
the word columba (dove) is only less
tailored for the bird than the Spanish form paloma
haunts us in Yradier's cooing song:

Sia tu ventana llega una paloma,
trattala con cariño qu'es mi persona;
cuentala tus amores bien de mi vida,
corona la de flores qu'es cosa mia!

But the plover in pigeon form, the dove no song,
no lover landing on his lady's window
in form of dove to be lovingly carressed,
wreathed with flowers and whisperingly told
her secret desires (as the god of love himself,
the winged Eros, by his Psyche landed),
the real dove of ornithology,
no poet's dream of love, but hungry birds
quick to quarrel, none of your peace symbols,
all two hundred and ninety species of them
(all ascended plovers on this Tree),
souls that wear the body of a dove
(like Paolo and Francesca, those lost doves)
although of peace no symbols, are so of love
(all of them mate for life and all the spouses
bill and coo and pet and fuss like fawners)
properly sacred to that glorious goddess
Aphrodite, queen of love and beauty,
she whose lovers all we poets are.

Impossible even touch on all the species
from the poor Mauritian dodo done to death
by man and his domesticated beasts
to the collared doves now taking over Britain
(Lorentz saw one eat her mate alive) –
a mint of hues from the Life-artist's palette.
The near-extinct Samoan tooth-billed pigeon
black and chestnut coloured with red legs;
the common rock dove from which all our tame

and semi-domestic pigeons are descended;
the cushat or ring dove ('wild wood dove') that Hopkins
saw as his emblem of the Peace of Christ
that would not round him roaming end, and under
be his boughs; the stock-dove whose echo
resounds through Robert's Afton Water;
the turtle-dove sung by so many poets,
she of the helio gown and oboe voice
(as beautiful a velvet sound as ever
luscious Delilah crooned in her Samson's ear);
the magnolia collared doves grace my own trees;
our own street pigeons (now five thousand years
associated with the human race);
and all those gorgeous doves of foreign lands –
the wedge-tailed green of Indonesia
(yellowish green and pink, maroon and crimson,
one of the great horde of fruit-eating pigeons);
the superb fruit pigeon of Australasia
(green and pink with succulent berry purples);
the magnificent (all green and wine and yellow);
the green imperial pigeon (greens and blues
and bronzes, lavender grey, chestnut and crimson);
the snow pigeon breeding on Everest;
cuckoo-tailed brown pigeons of the forest;
the brown and pink and violet mourning dove
(whose tail's like the murdered US passenger pigeon)
widespread in the States and Mexico;
the shell-grey Inca dove with russet wings;
the brilliant emerald dove of the bamboo forests;
the bleeding-heart (with white breast splashed with red);
the Nicobar, with its giant dark green mane;
and biggest of all, New Guinea's crowned pigeon
(with bluegray lace mantilla on the head)
hunted by vicious man for its lovely feathers,
large as pheasants, doomed by human bitches.

But no mellifluous Mexican peon song
(as far's I know) is written of the sandgrouse,
the pin-tailed form of north-east India,
the Pallas's (from wisdom's goddess named?)
or any of the other fourteen species:

pigeons resembling grouse in shape and habits,
eremitic birds, all fond of deserts
rootling about in wastes for seeds and such,
power-winged for necessary ranging
in search of food and water in such country.
Their chicks, who peck but cannot fly, are said
to drink water from the drenched parental feathers
(more likely they get water from the crop).
These souls at times go mad with arid living
and flee to richer realms – only to die.

(45)

The raven of the bens (and Edgar Poe)
has relatives of course among the crows:
but who but bird men'd sire on it a legion
includes the parrots, plantain-eaters, cuckoos,
rollers, bee-eaters, kingfishers and owls,
nightjars, swifts, humming-birds and colies,
trogons, barbets, jacamars and toucans –
even indeed all perching birds, the finches,
thrushes, chatterers, broadbills, manakins,
lyrebirds, swallows, buntings, warblers, wrens,
tanagers, wagtails, orioles, larks and pipits,
woodpeckers, tits, flycatchers and babblers –
enough! The Lord High Everything else of birds.
Yet this they say is anatomical fact.

But round the Amazon the hoatzin
(another *happax legomenon* of a bird,
like them all from archaeopteryx descended
only more so), part rail, part game-bird, part
a touracou, wholly only itself,
flaps about the trees above the rivers,
ring-dove sized, but as archaeopteryx
with lengthy tail, and born a quadruped.
The hoatzin can climb with all four limbs,
dive and swim if need be (falling from bough)
and climb the tree again; digests in the crop;
baffling in many ways the pigeon-holers.

Touracous (or plantain-eaters) show
similar links with the archaeopteryx
(as do, in lesser ways, even the pheasants):
the chicks reveal their lizard ancestry.
To Africa confined, two dozen species,
these long-tailed, crested birds whose outer toes
can function fore and aft (like all this clan),
eat tamarinds, bananas, paw-paws, plantains;
their colours (like so many other birds)
a painter's dream of visual paradise.
And from their wings a certain pigment's got,

of crimson-copper colour, called turacin:
both from the red-winged kinds who keep to forests
(the great blue, the violet, the blue-crested)
and the plainer kinds, like the grey, and the one that shout
'go away', that haunt the bush and savannah.

The cuckoos and associated birds
bridge across from touracou to parrot,
all with yoke-toed feet (two front, two back,
as needed), all eccentrics in their life-styles:
cuckoos, anis, roadrunners, couas and coucals –
a hundred and thirty kinds of Montmartre drop-outs!
The cuckoos proper, the common, the spotted, the bronze
(thirty-seven species it is said)
sung by the poets and frowned upon by husbands
swylce geac monath, geoman reorde,
singeth sumeres weard, sorge beodeth
bittre in breosthord, as Seafarer hath it),
the plaintive cuckoo calling with dreary voice
in summertime boding sorrow for some
poor creatures, bitterness for the heart –
for cuckolded husbands (bringing up other men's children),
for many a nestling murdered by young cuckoos,
for parent birds enslaved by the usurper.
Is it because the parent cuckoos cannot
stand our climate long enough for rearing
but must be off before the young are ready,
that thus they exploit the instincts of their betters?
Or is it excess of males and polyandry?
And those migrations of the amazing young
alone, long after the adults have flown, to climes
far south, with no experienced leader!
Nature makes miracles out of delinquency,
careless of human notions of good and evil.
And how can cuckoos camouflage their eggs
to look like those of various conscript hosts?
Even the gape of young cuckoos can be
imitative of the host-bird's nestlings.

Of *im*proper cuckoos (Lord, what cuckoo isn't?)
the malecho breeds of both Old World and New,

the black-billed, yellow-billed, scalefeathered,
build their own nests, and bring up their own young
(definitely not quite U my dear –
such things are always best left to the servants);
and as for the anis of the American tropics
(a raffish gang of Bohemian loose-livers
living and nesting in anarchic communes)
what self-respecting cuckoo'd talk to them?
America, too (home of rebels), houses
those ground cuckoos (Malaya has some others)
called roadrunners (though it must be said
the striped kind, the pheasant, and pavonine
have learned to dump their eggs like all true cuckoos).
The couas of Madagascar (like roadrunners)
do the family duties for themselves,
sociable as Glasgow picnic parties
(if less vulgar), some delicate and rare
as Delalande's coua (query extinct).
The Earth for rare birds gets daily tighter.
These menial habits (in cuckoos far too common)
are common too among the clan of coucals,
curious birds of the Indo-Pacific area,
Australia, Solomons, Africa, New Guinea,
primitive as aborigines
and as wonderful disappearers in the bush
on which they sometimes sprawl like some old rags,
and in which they build their nests that look
like long-necked basket-bottles on their sides,
with the neck a tunnel entrance to the nest.
Sometimes in the indigo Kenya night
(alive with all the din that Milton ever
could conceive in Pandemonium)
you'll hear the contralto burble of the coucal.

(46)

The fabulous Tree of Life that Nature grows
so trunks and branches, twigs and ramifies
and leafs and flowers, that no forest tree,
be it ever so high, so rich, complex and glorious,
is other than to this a wispy paradigm,
a lighthouse beam on a glorious summer day.
As over-eating kills as dead as hunger,
as surfeit of love's as bad as deprivation
and too much wealth's as evil as too little,
so too much wonder, poetry, gluts the sense
and too much admiration stuns the mind.
Even the busiest bee must sometime rest,
the sturdiest mind and body still need sleep:
and life must have night as well as day.

Here is no luscious syrop of young lover's
hymn to his mistress or the Delilah moon,
no metaphysical's dance of verbal wit,
philosophy's wisdom, the poet's frenzied eye,
the troubling of the well of inspiration,
Olympian calm of high imagination,
Orpheus' lute and spell-binding song:
all wonderful things, and well I know it
who've drunk my heady wine at all these fountains.
Yet though this poetry's of fact and not invention
I think my real Muse is no less fair
'than any she belies with false compare'.
And to put it as directly as I can,
a poetry of fact can only be
achieved if the fact itself is poetry
through which is clearly seen Life's miracles.
To me no poetry does, or ever can
come near the poetry that Nature is,
and my task here is not so much to get
in verse that multifoliate miracle
as, keeping out of its way, to let it be:
this poem whose muscular verbs are lives in action,
whose nouns are creatures, whose every name's a song.

This marks at least a break with bourgeois verse
conceived of as some individual myth
private to poets for their own salvation
not as Man, but as individualist:
a good bourgois, making spiritual money.
'What do you do?' (professor to me at a party)
'I write verse' (quietly I reply).
'but what do you do for SOCIETY, I mean'.
Great Sun in heaven, O holy Mother Earth,
what better for *society* could I do
than write its poems for it, physic its ills?
Not those phoney poems flatter its ego,
encourage it to drown in its illusions
(the kind that bolster rank establishments up,
win poetry prizes, fame, or laureation)
but the real poems that lance the abscesses,
expose death and its workers for extinction,
disinfect infections, purge the poisons,
restore man to Nature, Nature to man:
poems explode society's false values,
poems that hymn the mystery of life –
damning profiteers and usurers
but venerating the salmon leaps the falls.
Is not the Tree of Life the Tree of Health?

The truth of poetry, the poetry of truth
(a 'romance that's also true', John Barbour said
of his epic on the life of Robert Bruce)
is surely the supremest aim of verse.
What else have our best poets tried to do
but set in verse what they believed was true?

(47)

To touracous and cuckoos near related
(who knows how), the vast clan of parrots,
a riot of colourful tumblers, takes the stage
cascading into a circus: nutcracker-faced
macaws and cockatoos, parrakeets
and budgerigars, the lovebirds and the lories,
animals with skulls like no other birds
(but with powder-downs like the cranes and herons).
yoke-toed, with two toes front, two back.

Oldest (perhaps) of all these parrot forms
is New Zealand's owl-parrot, or kakapa,
a green and yellow, forest-coloured bird
that hides in holes by day and feeds on berries,
another bird that's lost the power of flight
and taken to earthier forms of foe-evasion,
nesting in burrows and under roots of trees
like other of the ground-reverting species.

How many kinds? Far too many hundreds
to even mention, their chief home grounds
Malaya, South America, Australasia,
and in India and Africa a few:
but the red-tailed grey, our commonest cage-parrot,
homes (when in the wild) in West Africa,
using feet (like them all) as hands for eating –
raucous, whistling, exhibitionist birds
who mimic human voices with distinction.
Some of them even learn to count to seven
and deal with knotty intellectual problems
(or practical ones like picking complex locks).
Strangest of all, these birds (essentially wild)
can lap up and return human affection
and even slily repay injuries.

Their tongues divide these birds in two main groups:
those whose tongues are blunt and feed on nuts,
and the brush-tongued ones that feed on juice and nectar.
Nearly all of them nest in holes and trees

and mate if not for life at least for years.
In size they almost span the Aves range,
some smaller than goldcrests, others larger
(from tip to tail) than golden or other eagles,
most, in colour, dominantly green.
Australia has the largest tribe of parrots
(too many for the bank-books of fruit farmers):
white, and rosy cockatoos, lories
(nectar-feeding), and bustling lorikeets,
parakeets and budgerigars and lovebirds.
Papua, New Guinea and other islands
have their colour-trove of these bright treasures;
New Zealand has, as well as its kakapa,
the kea, which has taken to sheep-stealing,
tearing the living flesh (at times to the kidneys)
killing the passive sufferer in the process.
Nature in the raw is never mild:
neither (for no good reason) is human nature.
The kea only kills in desperation,
hunger-driven in winter from the mountains
to forage on the outskirts of sheep stations,
large as any raven and as deadly.

Its less horrific relative, the kaka,
(a favourite pet from early Maori times)
bred in milder climes, has fruit in plenty.
Pygmy parrots, under three inches long,
inhabit New Guinea, New Ireland and New Britain,
stiff-tailed as tree-creepers (or woodpeckers),
blobs of colour dripping from Life's brush,
nesting (intrepid souls) in termite houses,
sure that wasps and bees won't dare usurp them
(as they do nests in other tropical parts).

South America's macaws surpass
all others for size and weight of body and bill
made to crack such problems as Brazil nuts,
riotous coloured as all but few of them are,
a brilliant tropical extravaganza.
Lovebirds of course appear to earn their name,
together rapt in some erotic dream:
on tiptoe therefore let us steal away.

(48)

This weird order of so-called raven forms
throws up a rag-bag next of birdly beauties:
rollers, bee-eaters, hoopoes, kingfishers, hornbills,
owls, nightjars, swifts and humming-birds,
colies, trogons, barbets, toucans and woodpeckers –
O Mystery, thy name's taxonomy!

Kirombo roller of Comoro Islands
(ancientest of all the clan of rollers)
tu-hou-tu-hou-tu-houing, in air hovering
or plunging down, grey-green-coppery red
with white belly and lumbar powder-downs
to feed on daylight lizards and grasshoppers.
The score or so species of roller proper,
blues and green and reds and browns, tumbling
and twisting about in the bird-resistant air,
jaylike in form and ravenlike in voice
(aerial gymnasts in bright Pallio costumes)
centre on Africa, though spreading wider:
at Berwick I've seen two on telephone wires.
But in Madagascar their ground-roller cousins
haunting the dusks of sunset and of dawning,
shy and elusive, have no yen to wander;
round-winged, long-legged birds of the undergrowth
(five species in all) and all ground-feeders.

South America (up to Mexico)
is motmot country, birds with racket-tails
but quiet of habits, hiding in tropical forests,
greens and turquoise blues their dominant colours,
bill serrated for butchering of insects.
Solitary birds (or territorial pairs),
they space themselves out in half-mile patches,
tunnelling in banks in the nesting season,
both sexes brooding in self-fouled nests.

But in Cuba, the Isle of Pines, Puerto Rico
Hispaniola, Jamaica and such isles,
the tiny todies run to five species.

splashes of colour, greens, off-whites and reds,
incessant chirmers (like European goldcrests)
tunnelling out burrows to lay their eggs in
(eggs the eye can all but see right through).
They lead a highway robber life with insects,
dashing from hideouts to lug them back as prey.

(49)

Halcyon, king Poseidon's beautiful daughter
garbed in assorted seaweed colours, threw
herself in ocean after her drowned Ceyx:
both were made kingfishers by the gods,
the *mimnomen alcyones* (of Sidon's Antipater)
who with nereids mourned Corinth's destruction.
Thus the poet: but the ornithologists tell
a tale more wonderful and as beautiful
of the real kingfishers in their seaweed gowns
flashing with iridesce as no seaweed does,
the alcyones family of a hundred and fifty
varied species; weak-legged, spear-billed birds
with bound front toes and lengthy keels,
in two main septs: the older wood-kingfishers,
and the water ones we all today know best.
These wood-kingfishers haunt the shady forest
eating insects, molluscs, reptiles, frogs
and sometimes fish; but the sept also boasts
Australasia's burbling kookaburra,
the shoe-billed species of New Guinea (large
and top-heavy), and other less-known species.

Our own bright jewel, spirit of shy streams,
the Halcyon and Ceyx myth outmarvels
(though they bring no halcyon days preventing winds
from troubling the nests they never build on the waves):
their nestlings take their turn in strict rotation
to feed from the beak of the returning parent.
Most of these birds are flying colour-schemes:
the striped, the belted, the racket-tailed, the hook-billed,
the lizard-eating, sacred, Indian stork-billed,
the worm-eating giant of New Guinea mountains,
the orange-purple-black, vermilion-billed,
three-toed kingfisher of south-east Asia –
some of the colour-schemes duller than others.

The bea-eater clan, little less colourful,
some thirty-five species (averaged blackbird size)
are highway robbers (like the todies and others)

dashing from favoured hide, returning to it
prey fast in aristocratic beak.
Their swallow flight over Abyssinia
and other such places (even, rarely, Britain),
their burrowing and tunnelling for nesting
traditional in all this avian group.

Rome station is the only (unlikely) place
where I have seen a hoopoe, flying under
the tall arcades of glass, unable to exit,
not flying low enough to find the outlets.
I watched with anxious, helpless eyes
(aware of Man's responsibility),
but time and a waiting train pulled me away
from any hope of helping this poor brother
trapped in our unnatural construction.
I caught my train, but still I can declare
not only I but all our human kind
no greater purpose have, nor can on Earth
(unless it's building stations they can live in),
than freeing hoopoes from our railway stations.
Was this bird's plight for the sins of Tereus
who raped Philomela and cut her tongue out
lest she disclose the deed (as the poets tell),
still hounded by the furies down the ages
and even put through hell in railway stations?
But hoopoe, this 'upupa' and four others
(curiously barred and helmeted because
in danger it flops aground like coloured rags),
is it the curse also on Tereus
that makes it eat dung-beetles, foul its own nest?

The wood-hoopoes of Africa alone
are cousins of the rascal Tereus
but lack (I hope) such skeletons in the cupboard
as Philomel, Procne, and poor little Itylus
(the nightingale, the swallow, the roasted pheasant
served by those sisters up for his father's dinner):
a less extravagant bird, of quiet ways,
dress, and quite a model parent it is said.

Hoopoe to hornbill seems a mighty leap
but anatomists simply step across,
assuring us they're all but first cousins
in this vast interlinking family tree.
Some forty-five species of this big-nosed lot
that grace with their colourful presence many lands –
Africa, India, the Philippines, Malaysia
New Guinea, the Bismarck and the Solomon Islands –
many of them with eyelashes, like mammals,
some as small as pigeons, others condor size,
with wavy, porpoise flight on hissing wings,
at times in squadrons (definitely raffish)
braying and honking rustily as they go.
Fruit and berries, insects, even mammals,
indeed they'll eat near anything that comes
including poisonous seed some fruits contain.
But the marvel of the hornbill's hir nesting,
the female immured in a cavity of mud
with only a slit for her bill so that the male
can feed her with his half-digested food
parcelled in the lining of his stomach
(which he regrows that she may feed again):
by the time she breaks out from her self-made jail
(having moulted and re-feathered in confinement)
the sacrificial male is like to die.
One by one the chicks too break out
and after each the nest's walled up again:
so it is at least with certain species.
New Guinea natives venerate such birds,
their spirit-houses deck with hornbill totems:
they even tame and take them about as pets.

(50)

One day in my boyhood in St. Andrews
I climbed a derelict cottage to the roof
and down the chimney saw stare up at me
the loveliest bird that I had ever seen,
a white-breast barn owl, heart-faced, huge of eye,
and held my breath in wonder at the sight:
a week later the nest was full of bricks,
as my heart was with anger, pity, hate.
Another day I came out of the Bute
in wintry dusk with D'Arcy, and we saw
a tawny owl I came to know quite well
(it roosted in St. Mary's College oak)
silhouetted on a nearby bush.
For me still the owls are beautiful
with a different beauty from all other birds:
the down-pile plumage, the glorious eyes,
eyes of genius (Goethe, Burns, Beethoven)
bowls of light that know all joy and pain.

The snowy owl for instance – how describe
that Persian-cat-like goddess of the arctic?
The kinds of barn-owl, long-eared, short-eared owls,
such lesser known ones as the scops, the eagle,
the little owls, the pygmies, Tengmalm's owl,
the burrowing owl of South America,
the fishing owls of Africa and Asia
that snatch up fish from the surfaces of lakes;
the great horned owls, the Lapp, the elf,
spectacled owls, the hawk owls (hard of plumage),
over a hundred and thirty kinds in all.
We tend to think of them as hawks of the night,
but they are of a wholly different race
allied to swifts and nightjars, not to falcons,
and all of them with forward-looking eyes,
bold to attack molesters of their young.
No wonder that, with their exquisite taste,
the Greeks made owls the sacred birds of Pallas.

Between these owls and the (so-called) goat-sucker clan

of nightjars, comes the oil-bird or guacharo
of Trinidad and other American tropics:
a brownish, crow-sized bird that lives on fruit
plucked at night after its cave-dwelling day.
Natives harvest the young for food and oil
they use in cooking, and to burn in lamps.
Their next of kin, the frogmouths, are like owls
evolving slowly into something else
(perhaps to nightjars?), but with sizeable powder-downs,
their food more like the owls' than the guacharo's:
inhabitants of Australia, Papua,
India, Malaya, Borneo and the like.

The eighty species of the nightjars proper
(including potoos) range the world over,
birds that seem to be made of the barks of trees
into which they merge in camouflage,
birds of the night and bat-time, mid-air feeding
(huge mouths gaping) like nocturnal swifts:
they never perch, but lie along tree-branches.
Our own nightjar is called fern-owl in places:
but in Brazil and Argentina are
kinds that fly long streamers from their wings
the pennant-winged nightjar for instance, and
the standard-winged; while certain African kinds
have streamer tails – God alone knows why
except that Nature loves extravagance,
coloratura styles, display of riches:
Nature likes to cock a snook at logic,
peacock it, paradise-bird it, out of pride.
But who can see such treasures in the dark?
Maybe, though, these floutings indicate
comparative security of life,
like fancy curtains flounced in suburban windows.
Some nightjars hibernate – rare trait among birds.

But O those tearaway, black-suited boys
of our too few summer days, the skirling swifts
who roar down evening streets on sickle wings
then soar up and zig-zag about the sky,
like Dis's squads tracking Persephone,
(too long absent from his umbrous halls)

to drag her down again, and with her, summer.
Sooty kin of the nightjars (not of swallows)
these paragons of helter-skelter flight
in sharp contrast to gliding albatrosses
(air force fighters compared with great air liners)
symbolise to me both hope and fear;
but in themselves, freedom itself they are.
They spend more life in air than other landbirds
feeding entirely on what the air provides,
landing rarely except in nesting season
(even mating's done upon the wing),
their nests litters of straw by saliva bound
and lined with a few feathers. The edible swift
whose nests make bird-nest soup in the far East
builds in vast colonies under the roofs
of vaulted caves, from Malasia to Australia,
nests of pure saliva (setting in air)
easily boiled down again for soup.
Collecting them from hundred-foot ladders
is an industry of importance in some countries,
though some are too adulterate for use.
The smallest nest of any living bird
is the one-and-a-half inch nest of the crested tree swift
of Papua, and some related places,
one-egg bearing, the mother overlapping,
the egg pure white (as all the eggs of swifts are)
from centuries of nesting in dark caves.
Like nightjars, and like certain humming-birds.
some swifts are capable of hibernation.

(51)

America's three hundred humming-birds
(close if strange, kindred of the swifts),
birds which specialise in hovering,
the Life-artist's genius in lyric mood
jewelling the forests with rare gems
of almost floricultural adornment,
tiny birds of brilliant hues that sport
banners, gorgets, shields, crests and tufts,
streamers, whiskers, plumes and pantaloons,
pendants and swaggering moustaches.
The oldest species seem to be the largest
(the giant, some nine inches), evolution
favouring the small (down to two inches):
some are little bigger than big hornets,
their beaks evolved from swift-beaks to probosci
of great length (and sometimes curvature)
for sounding the insides of long-belled flower,
hovering outside like helicopters
then darting quick as flashes to some other.
These birds, like the gods, eat mainly nectar,
though some catch flies and beetles on the wing.
Birds of the steaming equatorial forest?
Yes, and of Tierra del Fuega,
the Andes snowline, up to even Alaska:
they penetrate all parts and many climates,
but usually near their chosen prey —
the nectar-feeding insects and the flowers
their hovering technique's developed for.
Those rapid wing-beats make the humming sound;
the speed itself (as in bees) by special wing-joints.
Like helicopters, they fly in all directions,
their wings invisible to human sight,
and like insects too they pollinate some flowers.
These little birds are fearlessly aggressive,
fighting each other almost like jungle cocks
and even scaring mammals, hawks and snakes —
for its size the most pugnacious of all birds.

Polygamy the rule, some males build nests
not for use but as bower-birds build bowers
to attract the females who alone bring up the young:
but with so many species, many the variations
of rules and habits from the general.
Like the swifts, these birds use their saliva
to glue together miracles of nests
(sometimes on glassy slopes or under leaves)
camouflaging them with bark and lichen:
some are baskets hanging on a string.
Impossible to detail hundreds of species:
one can but write a lyric poem of names –
the sickle-billed hummingbird, Andean rainbow,
white-footed racket-tail, the heavenly sylph,
the rufous hummingbird, the sun-angel,
the ruby-throated, the frilled coquette of Brazil,
the Comte-de-Paris' star-frontlet, the bee,
the Sappho comet, the graceful train-bearer,
helmet-crest, the violet ear, the long-tailed
hermit, the sapphire-wing, the plover-crest,
Princess Helena's coquette, the racket-tailed,
the sabre-wings – one could go on and on
but man shall not live on plum duff alone.

Colies of South Africa, those mousebirds
distantly related to the swifts
(nine wee twigs of this great singing tree)
are mousy in their colouring as well,
with long mouse-tails (but unmousy crests)
poor fliers (in bush too dense for flight)
they creep about the trees like little mice,
feeding not on insects but on fruit,
and roost like bats (and certain of the parrots)
hanging upside down by small red feet.

Beautiful bronze-green quetzel of the trogons,
crested like the hoplite, strawberry-bellied,
over a yard in length of avian splendour,
streamer tail often tipped with blue,
you out-paradise birds of paradise
in Central America's misty mountain forests.

But for all your bravery of plume and colour,
like Milton you take on the lowliest duties
equally shared with your not so glorious mate.
Like him too, you're a soul apart
for though (with India and Africa) there are
some two score trogon species in the world,
the family's apart from other birds
and may indeed be slowly dying out,
with delicate skins and feathers easily lost.

(52)

Little jacamars of American tropics
seem to bridge the kingfishers and perchers,
sept of a pecking clan includes woodpeckers.
The Tree of Life's no ladder but a rambler
and here the interweaving gets more puzzling
for they relate too with the puff-birds and
the barbets, not to say with gross-billed toucans.
Fourteen species, goldfinch size to pigeon,
burnished jewels of brilliant reds and bronzes,
insect-hawks, though not as fast's the swallow,
out they dart from ambush on their prey,
bearing it back again to make a meal of.
They drill out holes in banks for nesting,
as do their nearest kin the silly puff-birds
who stand around and just let hunter shoot them:
jacamar-sized birds with flouncy heads
which can be puffed out hugely – hence the name:
some thirty species, all tropicamerican.

The metal-clinking barbets, Old and New World
busty birds that not only sound but look
like blacksmiths bred to the anvil and the forge,
most numerous in Africa, with only
twelve of some eighty species American.
Kin of the toucans and the honey-guides,
they have a garish tough-guy style and stance,
heavy-billed and bristly (hence the beard-name)
gutsing on paw-paws, guanas, berries, insects,
nesting in holes like woodpeckers, or burrows.
One, the gold-rumped tinker-bird, is often
cuckolded by certain honey-guides
whose chick kills off the luckless barbet chicks
with a special spike (which soon drops off) on its beak,
but still is cared for by the foster-parents.
Greenfinch-sized to that of jay or jackdaw,
they heavily bob about thin upper branches,
mostly blending in with bright green plumage,
or (like woodpeckers) belabour the air in flight.
Some kinds are found in circum-tropical Asia,

China, Malaysia, Ceylon, the philippines;
the coppersmith barbet (or crimson-breasted)
chief among them (one of the smallest of them)
haunting the tallest trees of town and village;
while one of the biggest, the great Himalayan barbet,
loudly laments high up those skyscraping mountains.

The curious shifts that creatures take for living
(among them symbiotic interweaving)
the honey-guides incomparably instance.
Unable themselves to penetrate the bee-hive,
from which some kinds desire beeswax and grubs,
they waylay honey-ratels and black hunters
and chatteringly guide them to a hive
(not necessarily known to them beforehand),
sometimes even flying at their faces
to pull them back from taking a wrong direction.
The hive discovered, the ratel breaks it open
(or the man, protected by a smoking faggot)
and the honey-guide garners its percentage –
one of few creatures able to digest beeswax.
The greater honey-guide and the scaly-throated
(cousins and cuckolders of the barbets),
dull-plumed birds about the size of thrushes,
seem to be the species most involved
(out of some eleven recognised).

As hornbills to the Old World, toucans to the New
if only in appearance (though they lack a casque)
for it's with barbets their anatomy belongs.
Those huge beaks in fact are very light
and are a highly special adaptation
for reaching succulent fruits on twigs so fragile
they could not bear the full weight of the bird:
not meant, as in the parrots, for heavy work.
Denizens mainly of Amazonia and
the lower Andes, sporting their blacks and yellows,
blues and reds and orange, among the tree-tops
where branchery is delicate and weak,
tossing and gulping down the fruits they pluck,
and racheting (like hornbills) on the wing:

a noisy, squabbling colloquy of souls
(in many ways like much more colourful rooks).
Near forty species here and there there are:
emerald toucans, keel-billed, laminated,
chestnut-mandibled toucan of the isle
of Barro Colorado in Panama,
the curl-crested, the tribe of aracaris –
some of them make entertaining pets.

What harm have Madagascar, Australia, done
(not to mention many a South Seas isle)
that they woodpeckerless should have to live?
Is it because they're so immensely rich
in other creatures found in them alone?
Or is it that such paradisal isles
need no such further gifts of heavenly grace?
More than two hundred species (counting the wrynecks
and the piculets) bless the woods
of most other countries in the world:
cousins of toucans, jacamars and barbets
(also hole-nesting birds that lay white eggs),
with spiny tails to sit on, with chisel bills,
extensible, almost chameleon tongues
(as toucans too have) with saliva sticky
to help them feed on beetles, ants and such.
Woodpeckers proper drill their own nest-holes,
the male doing most of the work (as of chick-rearing).
Some of the clan seek ants upon the ground:
the ground woodpecker of South Africa
and the little birds called flickers in the States
(diminutive woodpeckers, eating off the ground).
Others, the sapsuckers, are precisely that,
though they get their fill of insects with the sap
which gathers in the holes or grooves they dig,
our own green yaffle one among them:
and some of the species feed on eggs and chicks.

The piculets are almost thirty species
(one in Africa, three in south-east Asia
and all the rest in tropicamerica)
most of them about the size of warblers

with soft tails and other features like
(last of the clan, most primitive of all)
the wrynecks (two nightjar-coloured species),
ground-eaters of ants, like green woodpeckers,
but nesting in discovered holes in trees.

(53)

This mighty singing branch of the Tree of Life
here sprouts in myriads twigs at the twittering top,
five or six thousand kinds of perching birds
(all, it seems, in the archetype of raven)
mostly having special sound-box throats,
vocal organs made of a reedy syrinx
by which the heights of song can be ascended
by avian divas like the nightingale,
the lark, the blackbird, warblers and the song-thrush –
three quarters of the world's bird species,
the seraphim of the earthly paradise.

Broadbills of the Indo-Malaysian forests,
third and fourth toes bound (as in the nightjars)
seem to be the oldest of this order;
vegetarians, insect-eaters, often
beautiful birds (sparrow to pigeon size)
building oval nests or eel-like baskets
(usually hanging over rivers or pools).

South America's chatterers can boast
some of the strangest, loveliest birds alive:
take the flaming orange cock-o-the-rock,
the black umbrella bird with its great crest
(Victorian muff or tea-cosy on the head),
the snow-white bell-bird (alias campañero)
who wears on his head (like the horn of unicorn)
a wattle that's erectile like a penis
which, when erect, calls forth its peals of triumph:
some (to heap a trifle on plum pudding)
add two more such phalloi, on each temple.
South America too has manakins
haunting the undergrowth around the swamps,
the males dancing together in courtship dance:
seventy species (is it?) rich profusion
of beautiful little cameos of creatures.

Tyrant-birds, more awesome in name than deed,
in fact are just American flycatchers

(though in some ways they adumbrate the shrikes)
a mere four hundred species it is said
(if you doubt my figures count them for yourself)
but some like swallows forked in tail:
best known is the king-bird, crowned with fire –
a bird of quite heroic deeds of courage.

Ant-thrushes (or jewel-thrushes or pittas)
don't eat ants, neither are they thrushes
(which won't surprise sojourners in this kingdom)
but birds which hunt for insects on the ground
under the undergrowth of dense jungles,
ants a very small part of their diet.
Some are more like chatterers than thrushes.

Tapacolas, ant-birds and wood-hewers
(with bush wrens) are a voice-box departure
from previous birds towards the greatest singers
(the anatomical details I will spare you
and myself, though grateful to the scholars).
Little wren-like tapacolas hopping
on boughs, or running South America over:
wood-hewers (how many species?) dull birds
like all this lot, woodpecker-like in form,
some of them (like the firewood-gatherer)
build a complex nest of sticks and grass
(big enough at times to fill a barrow)
with a long lobby leading to the chamber:
oven-birds that build great globes of clay:
bush wrens (peculiar to New Zealand)
but four species in all, mere sidesprigs (like
the tapacolas) of the twigs of the singing tree –
most, like the rifleman, insect-eaters.

Madagascar (treasure-house of species)
has four little birds they call asites:
two of them like sunbirds (and once so called)
the other two like the jewel-thrush or pitta.

(54)

The lyre-birds are the first of a great tribe
(numbering five thousand kinds or more)
identified by the same kind of syrinx,
voice-box, spread the whole world over.
Their tail the lyre Apollo gave to Orpheus,
these gorgeous birds honour (unthanked) Australia,
dancing rather than singing for their mates
(each cock with his own bit of dancing ground)
on powerful ground-bird legs and digger claws;
two kinds (Superb and Albert) building oval nests
among the rocks and undergrowth of forests
diggers have brought a sling-shot from extinction.

Scrub-birds are abo Australians too,
abused (one of the two extinct?) like abos,
appreciated as little as the lyrebird;
ground-runners, with short and feeble wings,
they look like outsize wrens with longer tails.

Birds of paradise: the name implies
some notion of a realm no man has seen
and what it must be like if it exists –
a place of sensual ecstacies unknown
though glimpsed by men in their ecstatic moments
usually in sexual love-embrace,
as near to man-at-one-with-the-divine
as men can get. The mystics, even saints
describe in sexual terms their ecstacies,
for two at-one are also at-one with God.
The vulva are the gates of paradise.
Therefore these birds are innocent witnesses
(in name) to our true religion, Venus-worship.
Such angels of delight stream through the soul
only in moments of sublime orgasm
when the soul is re-united with the Life-God.

Angels? Some say these paradisal souls
are but crows in dandy feathers glorified:
they're not, of course, but birds of Earth they are

creatures of Nature like all other birds,
bearing like them (inside and out) be sure
the usual score or so of parasites.
New Guinea is a land of primal beauty
but nobody could call it paradise.
There it is these glorious birds are native
(over forty species, it is said)
some of their names as plummy as the birds:
the King of Saxony, the golden-silky,
paradise crow, King Albert's sickle-bill,
the curl-crested and trumpeter manucodes,
the six-wired bird of paradise and the twelve-wired,
the Hunstein's, the MacGregor, the superb,
the king, the wattled, the ribbon-tailed, the lesser,
the mocha-breasted, the magnificent riflebird,
Wallace's standard-winged, the several flagbirds,
the Emperor of Germany, the blue,
the red, the grey-breasted, the raggiana;
names Scheherezade might have used
to whisper in her murderous Caliph's ear.
Yet the panoply of flags and streamers, banners,
scimitars, sprays and semi-circles of feathers,
all that display of feathery pyrotechnics
outsplendouring the most refulgent splendours
of iridescent blues and greens and bronzes,
crimsons, purples, golds and blacks and yellows,
cascades and fountains of many-coloured plumage,
Nature's super-abundance – for what?
That cocks may find acceptance by the hens,
that nests may be built, eggs laid, chicks
be hatched and fed, grow up to replace their getters;
that what would happen anyway (even if
cocks and hens were plain as pigs) does happen.
Nature pours contempt on Occam's Razor.

The bower-birds of Australia and New Guinea
don't spend quite so much on fine feathers
but go to even more extravagance
to get females to what they'd do without
(like female toads and frogs and Komodo dragons)
by building fancy, often beautiful bowers

not for nesting but to impress the lady,
bowers decked and gemmed and even painted
with mosses, flowers, fruits, insects and pigments,
creative genius revelling in itself,
merely conscripting females as excuses.
Birds the average size of turtle doves,
are they close cousins of birds of paradise?
Gaudy birds expose themselves to danger,
a misplaced bravery: did the bower-bird
discover this safe substitute for plumage?
Once accepted, his hen builds her own nest
on more practical lines, a tool for living
rather than an ideal home for show:
and yet the bower really is a bower,
a love-nest for the mating of the lovers
(I've seen a photograph of one pair at it)
but not of course for bringing up the young.
True nests are often built (catbirds' for instance)
high up in trees, not (like the bowers) aground.

Wintering here with us in Edinburgh
beautiful extravert waxwings I have seen
boldly feeding under the Castle Cleuch
in Princes Street Gardens, bombycillidae
the classifiers call them (the birds with tails
of silkworm yellow) ignoring the roar of traffic,
squealing diesel trains and press of folk,
kin of swallows and shrikes (among other kinds)
silky flycatchers, palm-chats of West Indies,
the Persian (and such countries) hypocolius –
burdly birds, preferring the frosty north.

Their kin the swallows, flycatchers and shrikes
for us in our northern exile from the sunlands
mostly symbolise farewelling summers
and the heart's nostalgia for its native south.
Itylus of the steel-blue back and blood-splashed
throat, the callipers tail and creamy belly,
soaring and stooping, cecilia-voiced and sudden,
over and under the fleeting summer leaves:
grate-voiced house-martin, rumped and bellied with white,

building its miracle mudnest clamped to walls
and eaves with death-defying, fate-scorning daring;
tunnelling brown sand-martins as I've watched them
under the Braehead cliffs in old St. Andrews
by Hepburn's Wall and the Virgin of the Rocks kirk
(worshipped in before St. Rule was towered) –
these are but three of over seventy species
the bird men call the hirundinidae,
mostly close associates of men
and their adaptations of environments,
from Australasia up to the arctic circle.

Finest of fliers, the akin wood-swallows
(ten species from India to Australia)
tend to crowd together and sleep in clumps:
even, it's said, sharing communal nests.

Flycatchers wait (like puff-birds and others) in ambush
pouncing on passing prey and hiking it back
to the place of ambush (almost four hundred species
birds of the Old World only), some of them
(like the paradise flycatchers) birds of great beauty.

Cuckoo-shrikes, minivets of Asia, Australia
American greenlets, the clan of shrikes proper
impalers of beetles, lizards, mice and birds
on thorny larders for their later feeding,
sometimes alive, for their claws are too weak for crushing
Nature in the raw can outbutcher butchers.
Wood-shrikes (little like these butcher-birds)
racquet-tailed and other drongos, all,
with piping-crows, the others of this tribe,
mostly given to catching flies and insects.

(55)

Here in these top twigs of the Tree,
evolution ecstatic on the wing,
amoeba become a myriad sparks of birds,
I'm tempted to seek in *occupatio* refuge

(Here my Muse her wing maun couer,
Sic flichts are far ayont her pouer)

or in one great image to end all images
(as Dante did the beatific vision
in Neptune's awe at the shadow of the Argo).
But I'm no Dante, and I doubt if even he
could strike an image gathers in one rose
the thousand avian petals still unsung:
the daws, nutcrackers, New Zealand huia bird,
kokako, saddleback, the archetypes
of this whole legion of birds of raven form
the ravens, crows, magpies, choughs and jays,
the varga shrikes and such, the magpie-larks,
more than sixty chickadees, tits and verdins,
the bearded tit, nuthatches and tree-creepers,
the tribe of thrushes, bulbuls, babblers, chats,
true thrushes, redstarts, wheatears and accentors,
the shamas and the bluebirds, blackbirds and ousels,
the numberless varieties of warblers
(with the tailor-bird who stitches a nest of leaves),
vireas of the Americas and Indies,
goldcrests and kinglets and so many others:
the wrens and dippers (so-called water ousels)
the flower-bird clan of white-eyes, honey-eaters,
flower-peckers, sun-birds and honeysuckers
(whose plumes once decked the garb of Hawaiian kings)
the starlings and the golden orioles
including the grackle, yon chatterbox, or mynah,
the hang-nests of the Americas, which weave
Florence-flask nests hung from boughs or fibres;
caciques and cow-birds, the diva bobolink
(finest of all American singing birds):
hundreds of diglosses, tanagers
(those coloratura, all-American finches):

the Old World (and Australian) weaver-finches
building their retorts of basketry;
the weaver-birds who build one tenement mass
that houses hundreds of nests beneath one roof;
the widow-birds, glass-finches, Java sparrows,
the many kinds of grassfinches, mannikins, waxbills,
the clan of buntings and, above all, finches
one of which planted (as I suspect)
the seed of this poem when I was ten years old,
(a goldfinch coveted in a Glasgow pet-shop,
saved for through long weeks and longer months,
the subject of my earliest piece of verse –
a catalogue description of the bird),
bramblings, crossbills, reed and cirl buntings,
yellow-hammers, American cardinals,
larks, pipits, the bobbing band of wagtails:
a riotous wealth of lovely singing birds,
each and every one a feathered poem!
So many that my song is out of breath!

(56)

Dante (the latchet of whose bardic shoe ...)
took poetry (and mankind) as far from Earth
as it could go, took it up to the Sun:
starting from that common love, the Sun,
our way since then has led back to the Earth,
discovering that wife of our great Star
(whose love's the very livingness of life),
the Nature of our Earth and all her children.
So from the tree-tops where these birds have left me
I too must come down again to Earth
to meet our proper kind, the humble mammals.

The triumph of the forelimbs used as wings
implies what loss attendant on that gain?
What else can forelimbs do that may surpass
the glidings of the wandering albatross?
The albatross can't play a Bach Chorale
nor, by climbing trees, evolve a hand
to carve a Pieta, play a polonaise.
The Life-artist restlessly works out
new variations on the forelimbs theme,
what else can be done with jointed skeleton
of bone from where the reptiles left it,
bring new branches out on the Tree of Life.

As reptile scales in birds were changed to feathers,
so in mammals they give rise to hair:
the egg becomes a womb gestates the young,
the yolk-sac is replaced by a placenta,
the young are born alive, and instead of being
fed by the parents on part of their own food
are fed on milk secreted by the mother
in and from breasts (*mammae*) by suckling.
Mammals; the animals with breasts.
Like birds hot-blooded, four-chamber hearted,
a diaphragm that puts their breathing function
far in advance of other animals
(and 'breath' as we all know of course is 'spirit'),
so the way is cleared for a spiritual mammal

to do the most miraculous things with breath
(not only Caruso but the Nazarene):
and the mammal brain is also a real advance.

When first I caught an awed glimpse of this poem
looming up through reading of Erigena
on Nature's Divisions, twenty years ago
(his thought, to me sublime as still it is,
that all God's creatures are subsumed in Man,
Man in Christ and Christ in God the goal,
the final cause), I little knew just how
the animals are all in Man subsumed.
The way led me, before I earned the poem,
away from John's ninth century Christian view
through Darwin to to-day's biology
(of which I know only as much as, say,
our Scottish opera singers must of Italian).
Post-Dante European man
was forced to learn from life the truths of Nature
instead of weaving lies, like theologians.
All these years to get to this beginning,
tortured and battered each wrong inch of the way
by the hidden Real, till at last the veil was lifted
and I one morning woke with assurance talking
the opening lines that lead into this poem.
But Erigena, all that time ago
was vouchsafed a glimpse of evolution –
that Man sums up in essence all the creatures.

The earliest kinds of mammal still retain
traces of their gradual evolution:
the duck-billed platypus that still lays eggs
yet when the eggs hatch out, suckles the young:
the spiny echidna's little different
(and each has but one hole for voiding waste).
Only their Australian isolation
preserves these early mammals from extinction.
The kangaroos (most interesting of them all)
in whom gestation's rudimentary,
bear their young too foetal for independence,
yet able to crawl up to the marsupium

there to latch on a teat and live on milk
till, fully formed, they romp about as joeys.

This inner and outer uterus technique
is found in two or three hundred different species
in Australasia and America:
the kangaroos, wallabies, walleroos,
tree-kangaroos, the phalangers (with cuscus
flying-squirrels, koala bears and possums)
wombats, bandicoots, the dasyures
(Tasmanian wolf and devil, marsupial mice,
the thirty phascogales, banded ant-eaters
and marsupial moles), the true opossums
(how many kinds?) of all the Americas.
Some of them are dubbed 'two-wombed' (didelphic).

After these few links with the reptile stem
the mammals proper, all without exception
bring forth their young full-formed by the placenta,
many able to stand, suck for themselves
(mankind the most remarkable exception)
or even begin to forage their own fodder.
Most primitive are the toothless (more or less) lot:
ant-eaters, sloths, aardvarks and pangolins,
armadilloes, mostly short on fingers
and what they have little more than claws
to clutch at branches, tear the anthills open;
creatures of little brain or expectations,
burrowers in earth, keeping close the ground,
ponderous in body as in wit
these poor souls we still have with us,
like drop-outs hunched over dailies in public newsrooms.

(57)

The sirens that Ulysses listened to
singing of glorious breasts and yearning quims
(the 'eternal feminine leads us up and on')
an irresistible love-call to the male
who, bound to the marriage-mast, unable to follow,
knows such pain as Adam's exiled from Eden,
were not of course the sirens of to-day,
these manatees and dugongs of tidal waters
round Brazil, Australia, the Benin Bight
(nor Steller's late-exterminated sea-cow).
And yet these curious beasts can give, like seals,
some notion how the mermaid myth arose:
even their breasts are placed the same as women's.
Hence this order's given the name of sirens.

The manatees are roughly human size
(some bigger), coastal animals which reach
far up big rivers (even to the source it's said,
like over-grown salmon, of the Amazon itself):
dugongs are rather larger and sea-going,
while Steller's lost sea-cow reached twenty-five feet:
all descended from the same swamp beasts
as ancestored their cousin elephant.

Strange that that long labour to leave the sea
and colonize the land, swop gills for lungs,
trade fins for legs, and all that ache of growing,
should lead to the apostasy in some
of seeking again the oceanic life,
with legs instead of fins, lungs not gills,
yet find it worth, despite the handicap
of trying to reverse their evolution:
but so it is with many, not sirens only,
but whales and dolphins, seals, sea-lions, penguins.
The whales are far advanced in that regression,
hind-legs already feet-fluked, mermaid tails,
fore-legs flippers, ex-tail dorsal fin:
but still the lungs to gills have not reverted
and these great mammals have to copulate,

gestate, give birth and suckle as on land
where, unlike seals, polar bears and penguins,
on pain of death they dare no longer venture.
Nor can they fox whalers by keeping down
as long as need be to elude pursuers –
they must rise to breathe or drown, and when they do,
extinction's barbarous guns are there to slay
these tragic heroes trapped by a fatal flaw
which time could put right: if they *had* time.
Their fate depends on good men besting bad:
on which of course the fate of all Earth depends.

Beautiful baleen whales of gentlest nature,
straining the teeming ocean of its plankton
and other micro-life, easy as breathing,
some the largest mammals ever lived,
possible only in water (in which they're weightless)
countering the force of gravity.
No mammal could support such weight on land.
Right whales (right for whalers) of Greenland, Biscay,
pygmy right-whales of Australia, New Zealand,
grey whales of the Pacific, humpback rorquals
singing a half-hour aria under water
(repeating the whole) audible a hundred miles
(Nature's truth out-Disneys fantasy),
fin-whales (the true rorquals), the mighty blue
(over ninety feet at times in length)
all by man's improvidence sentenced to death
as many of the toothed whales also are:
unique and splendid creatures which, once lost,
like snowflakes on a stream are gone forever.
O God of Life, prevent such monstrous crimes!
Extirpate our evil money-systems!

Predatory whales armed with teeth
to grip or rend and chew, the cachalot
or sperm whale that Melville deified
(old whalers thought spermaceti was semen),
head a third of its length, the sperm cistern
helping withstand three thousand feet down pressure,
jaws to chew up giant squids (or boats)

swallow sharks, or men; an animal
magnanimous enough for Aristotle.

All these whales in birth produce one calf
already one-third grown; and I have seen
(exemplary of man's true role in Nature,
not destroyer of life but its preserver)
Cousteau's men move all but heaven and Earth
to save a stranded calf burned by the sun
and fed upon by gulls, even making milk
substitute to feed it on, mounting
twenty-four hour guard against the sharks.
I shared their grief when in spite of all, it died.
Yet Profit will, if allowed, wipe out whole species,
bull, cow, tenderest calves and all,
this *physeter macrocephalus* chief among them.

Some whales are little bigger than porpoises:
the pygmy sperm-whales, barely ten feet long,
in Indian water south-east to Australian
(Africa even, and the North Pacific):
the beak-whale clan with dolphin mandibles
geared for taking cuttlefish and such:
the bottle-nosed favours our north Atlantic:
Baird's or Annoux's whale, which haunts New Zealand:
the whales of Cuvier and Sowerby.

'Dolphins of my delight' George Barker sang
'gambading through bright hoops of days', those
beautiful mammals (not to be confused
with scombroid fish who're wrongly dolphins called),
the river kind of which do their gambading
mostly in South American river-mouths,
Rio la Plata giving their Latin name
of *platanistidae* – the Amazon inia,
Yangtse dolphin, the Indian Gengetic,
all fish-eaters, five to nine feet long.
The dolphins proper, such as I have seen
delightfully our troop-ships convoying
to and from the West African coast,
trundling days on end, cycling, wheeling

(as if the world had never heard of U-boats),
terror of flying-fish that skipped before them:
porpoises, as all of us have seen them,
sleek rubber tyres revolving in our bays,
our own little five-or-six foot whale:
killer-whale, the grampus (or the orc),
one of the most terrible beasts alive,
thirty feet of armed ferocity
whose specialty is prising whale-jaws open,
tearing out the tongue then leaving to die
an agonising death the wretched victim:
the rare and harmless false-killer whale (a black
creature with grampus teeth that lives on cuttles):
the pilot-whale (another of the smallest):
the white whale or beluga of the Arctic:
and that fantastic, unicorn-like beast
the narwhal, living not alone in legend
as you'd think but actually there in the Arctic,
flesh and blood with a spinal, rifled horn
sometimes nine feet long – for what?
All of them exotic mammals who
have turned their backs forever on the land
and, like the foaming wave, gone back to sea.

(58)

But from Earth's family let us turn a moment
to see Herself, our young and lovely Mother,
unique among the planets (if not in space)
in being Herself a living organism,
not only a blue-green jewel hung in space
but with atmosphere by living things created,
an air of oxygen by plants outbreathed
(both by land and sea) the Sun's garden,
His paradise, His darling bower of love –
Fertility, among Her barren sisters.
Not only life She bears but Life She is
(under Her inseminating Sun),
a living being made of living beings
as a living hive's composed of living bees,
Her every atom full of solar power.
How can we, Her creature sons and daughters,
honour, adore, worship Her enough,
this isle of life in a sterile sea of space,
this one oasis in a lifeless desert,
this warm igloo in an Arctic waste of ice?
Mother and wife and resurrecting tomb
from whom we spring forth, soar, descend and die
to be received and changed to other life
in this immortal spiral of creation –
how can we love and reverence Her enough?
And when we land men on the lunar wastes,
what is the greatest pleasure there they have?
To see their beautiful Mother in Her veils,
a lighted window in a midnight moor.
What greatest satisfaction do they gain?
To return to Earth and Her loving limbs once more.

We humans who break through to consciousness
of Earth's five billion years or so of being,
what are we conscious of but our position:
for are we not in fact but privileged
to be Earth's consciousness of Her own self,
to do Her work (and the Sun's), to be to all
our fellow-beings at least good neighbours,

unsentimentally caring, in terms of our nature,
for even those our lot it is to prey on?
Perhaps especially them, our tribal totems,
for even the air we breathe we get from others,
of life's interdependence at no point free.
The very soil's alive with organisms,
the air we breathe, the water that we drink,
the food we eat is so much vibrant life
and if it weren't, couldn't be our food;
for all that lives lives by the death of others.
Yet Life itself's immortal youth and love
though every living thing's an imminent death,
all us but clay in the Life-artist's hands.
Only the forms, the adaptations change
at evolution's pace (the real ones)
not the hysteric's chasing ephemeral fashions.

Man's biological growth ends with the Stone Age,
hasn't advanced in twelve million years.
What evolution's slow womb has formed
fashion-designers have no power to change,
though man's improvidence and sacrilege
can now destroy all that Earth creates,
even (blasphemy of blasphemies) Earth herself,
unless we can bring in time the market-place,
and the lunatic money-systems there enthroned
by vicious gangsters, under sane control:
make systems work for men, not men for systems.

We who should regard our nubile Earth
with the good bridegroom's passion for his bride,
using her, but lovingly and well,
his love a ministration as well's a feeling,
responsible for and to Her and Her children,
worshipping Her with body and (Her own) goods,
we in fact outrage Her with atom bombs
(Hiroshima, and the check-up Nagasaki),
pillage Her seams of minerals and oil,
pollute Her glorious, Her sacred air
with fall-out, petrol-fumes and other filth,
poison Her lakes and rivers, even Her oceans

with various abominable wastes,
hunt Her age-old species to extinction,
denude Her forests, lay waste Her soils
(spending in years the capital of aeons
that not even aeons ever can replace) –
and all for what? For the illusion of money,
man's slave become his God, for Profit,
the fast buck faster disappearing,
a few figures of fantasy in ledgers
falsely called Money; for mere ration-coupons.
Money was made that real goods might be
easily circulated among people,
not to hold each other up to ransom
for human needs the Earth gives free to all,
Nature's bounty, our legacy from the Sun.

What shall it profit a man if his Xanadu
is no sooner built than he loses the Earth it stands on?
Even self-interest – self-interest above all –
commands we treat our Earth with reverence.
The voice of God speaks clear through every science,
this world of Nature is our real bible
whose every living word's a word of God.

And as your Lord's last rays lip Arthur's hill
I too, but one of your sons, kiss you good-night
O beautiful Mother Earth, and thank you for being –
if only for the selfishest of reasons.

(59)

Talking of mothers, there's the humble cow
(symbol of Earth herself) the sacred cows
the Hindus do indeed call their mothers
(while we see them as dairies on the hoof),
live monuments to patient motherhood
and lifelong exploitation of the female:
mild, enduring beasts with fly-tormented,
sad eyes, unintelligent as big –
yet matadors will rather face a bull,
and when a breeder wants a fighting strain
it is the cows he tries out for their courage,
the bulls only for their stamina.

These ruminants whose life is chewing cud
time is thinning out, they're elegiac:
the wild ox or aurochs long has gone
from Europe, the bison lives on sufferance
and other species now we see in danger.
The gaur and banteng of Indo-Malaysia,
the Tibetan yak, survive – but for how long?
The Asiatic buffalo's presently safe
but the African may not have long to live
(like so many species) unless we intervene.
Hollow-horned and melancholy-voiced,
these creatures are akin to livelier beasts,
the various goats and sheep of many airts:
the mouflon of Sardinia-Corsica,
the red sheep found in Asia Minor,
the urials of mainly central Asia,
American bighorns, Asiatic argali,
the African arui (or Barbary sheep)
the true wild goats, the ibexes and markhors,
bharals, pasangs, the Himalayan tahrs
the chamois, serows, gorals and the takins:
their kin the musk-ox of the American arctic.

Among these creatures are those called 'antelope'
(a word first applied to the unicorn),
but these beasts plainly are no bloodless legend:

the Indian blackbuck, various hartebeests,
besboks, bonteboks, wildebeests
or gnus, the brindled gnu, not to say
American prongbuck and Rocky Mountain goats,
have been so-called, with African duikerboks,
klipspringers, grysboks, steinboks, suni, dik-diks
(beautiful mice-bucks perched on pencil legs)
reedbucks, waterbuck, defassas, kobs
and lechwes, oribis, dibatags, rheboks –
a jamboree of four-legged elegance
menaced by the threat to Africa's forest.
Lyre-horned impalas (pelted grace),
the unprepossessing saigas and the chirus,
loveliest of all, the lithe gazelles
(delicate symbols of sensibility)
forever torn to bits by thick-skinned brutes,
hyaenas, hunting-dogs, big cats and jackals
(sometimes, as in myself, within one soul).
Gerenuks, springboks (those bouncing-balls)
beira, gembucks and the oryxes,
addax, the roan and sable antelopes,
nyalas, bushbucks and the situtungas,
kudus, bongos, elands and the nilgai –
such treasures of living venison,
most of them threatened with final butchery.

All the mammals are in fact in danger
from the latest and most ruthless of them all,
Man, the arriviste, the social gangster,
penny-wise and pound-foolish, eyes
keen for the hare at his feet, horizon-blind.
I write this with a deep and dark foreboding
as one constrained to utter cries of warning.

Antelope-goats, the pundits choose to call
the two kinds of giraffe and the okapi,
creatures that look like some more normal beast
exaggerated by a distorting mirror,
or as if the Life-artist, in surreal mood,
had played about with geometric shapes
and finished off the works with action-painting.

Yet these fantasies in living flesh and blood
in fact, like all the other animals,
are walking biological equations
answer specific adaptation problems,
doing dumb-show take-offs of Joyce Grenfell.

(60)

Deor (simply 'beast' in Anglo-Saxon)
becomes for us the antlered beasts alone,
the deer (though Shakespeare used the broader form).
Reindeer of romance for Christmas children,
the real totem of the nomad Lapps
and Eskimo (to whom it's caribou),
a mild-eyed soul to whom mankind's in debt
(both as legend and as real provider)
only less than to cattle, sheep and goats,
pigs, and suchlike pastoral providers
(without whom I could not be writing this,
nor men be working to destory us all
rather than yield short-term to long-term gain),
distinguished from all other deer because
antlers are grown not only by males but females.

We Scots of course regard the red deer stag
almost as a national property
(as the red grouse really is) and certainly
as the golden eagle to birds, salmon to fish,
the red deer is king of all our mammals
(though the queen is the true leader, not the king).
More fools we, the way we treat all four.
The stag at eve still drinks his fill, but we
the people, gain little in mind or body from it
because he is the property of landlords
who stand between us and our heritage.
The roes and fallow deer are commoner
below the highland line, if only because
some enlightened landlords cultivate them
for their own sakes and not for wealthy guns.

But the deer of the wider world we only see
in zoos (which cannot but belittle Nature),
if at all – the great Pêre David's deer
of China (sometimes called mi-lu and sometimes
Ssu-ou-ksiang, the 'four unlikes', because
it has the tail of a donkey, a camel's neck,
cow's hooves, and the antlers of a stag),

which lives only in human parks and such.
No record of a wild one has survived.
The chitals of the Indian plains and foothills,
bamboo jungles, glades and purling streams:
the south-east Asian sambar, forest giant
haunting waters in dawn and evening twilight:
the sika of Manchuria and Japan:
Schomburghk's deer of Thailand's bush and plain:
the thamin or panolia of Malaysia:
the massive barasingha of Indian grasslands:
the Persian red deer (bigger than ours) or maral
and its Kashmiri kin the hangul stag:
that elk the Shawnee nation call wapiti
(biggest of living deer except the moose)
bugling among the giant mountain timber,
the rutting bulls in battle clashing like titans
while slier lovers lead the old bull's cows off.

America's white-tailed or Virginia deer
that fights and kills the lethal rattlesnake,
is one of many deer whose teeth are hollow:
mule deer too, home on its north-west range,
the sitka reaching north as far's Alaska,
black-tailed deer of British Columbia,
cariacu (or brocket) of Brazil,
huemals or tanugas of the Andes,
pampas deer, the little Chilean pudu
and the great marshdeer of South American swamps.
But in the end (of New and Old World deer),
we bow to his majesty, the Alaskan moose,
largest of all deer that still survive,
the sixteen-hundred pounder of the north,
his head too high on those long front legs
to reach the ground or grass without kneeling
or even to drink water without wading:
but for reaching into foliage they're like ladders.
How long will this great solitary beast,
monogamous by nature, Nature spare us?
How long, I mean, will we spare it to Nature?
How long, for the matter of that, will we spare ourselves?

Primitive musk-deer of the Himalayas
(hardy enough to stand Siberia even)
yielding perfume to the north Chinese
(from whom incredibly they hide in the tops of trees),
the douce little water deer of the Yangtse Kiang
(like the musk-deer wholly lacking antlers)
much like a hare and littering plural young:
barking deer (what deer, pray, doesn't bark?)
or muntjaks, hog-deer, jungle sheep, rib-faced deer,
for all their names are other delicate souls
brave in battle, much hunted for the pot.

These deer are small, but in the chevrotains
or so-called mice-deer (they're neither mice nor deer)
we see the smallest of the deer-like beasts,
some kinds weighing less than a small cat
or decent rabbit, easily tamed, able
to hang in trees by their canine teeth when hunted.

(61)

As ice to water, desert is to land:
and as the ice is caused by too much cold,
so are deserts made by too much heat
(though man's improvidence is threatening
to outdo the Sun and make all Earth a desert).
The Gobi and Sahara serve to warn
that even Earth can be made almost sterile,
that Life's a heritage that can be lost
and will, if man's present course continues.

Is it so strange that from the desert come
Yahwe and Allah, those sadistic gods
abominate the fertile goddesses
and over-rate mere masculinity?
That see love as a father-son affair,
ejecting woman from divinity –
believe a man will give birth to a saviour?
Can even deserts breed such wierd perversions
compared to which mirages are of Nature?
Surely here's the germ of Ezra's tale
of the operated sailor who was given
a whore's unwanted brat (just born next door),
solemnly told that it was found inside him,
and for the child became a millionaire,
confessing on his death-bed to his son
that he was not his father but his mother:
'your father was a merchant in Stamboul'.
What whore will bear the saviour for his 'mother'?

Deserts thus can give life curious kinks
and twists, forms as wierd's the ocean holds.
Therefore it need cause us no surprise
to see from deserts come the incredible camel,
a matted sea-serpent stuck up on legs,
all ups and downs and lurching side to side
(for even its gait perverts four-legged nature)
its vain semitic nose in constant sneer
elevated (as though in disdain of women),
its supercilious voice a cross between

a bored donkey and the House of Commons chorus,
spitting with contempt, long bearing grudges.
In spite of these aristocrat pretensions
he really is a prince of beasts of burden,
one to whom all mankind 's indebted;
if not handsome, hardy, fit to endure
unendurable toil in extremes of climate,
broiling days that end in freezing nights,
its three-part stomach geared for water-storing.

These Bactrian camels (this whole clan in fact),
the speedy one-humped (Arab) dromedary,
South American llamas and guanacos,
vicuñas and alpacas (all of them
sprung not from deserts but the Andes),
though dwindling wild ones here and there are found:
wild Bactrians in the Gobi, vicuñas and
guanacos in the Andes and such places.
On these pad-footed chewers of the cud
many vivid cultures have depended:
those of the middle-east, North Africa,
the Amerindian cultures – the Inca
held the vicuña dearer than human life.
Lacking them, Australia stuck in the Stone Age.

(62)

How long have men exploited the humble pig?
You may ask how long have men exploited fire:
anyway long before the earliest towns
Man's comradeship (a bit one-sided, true)
with pigs and other bosom animals
was well established – say at Eden's gates.
Are we not, we mammals, all one family,
even if a somewhat cannibal one?
Pigs through millennia have shared our house,
our bed, even the breasts our children sucked,
and still do in parts of the peasant world.
Man to certain cannibals was 'long pig'.
Swine, like the poor, we always have among us
as well as all our other animals.

Gruntle-nosed pig, rootling in undergrowth
or ploughing soft soil with upturned plate-snout,
you are no aesthete, though easily bruised,
ham-fisted lout, aye on the trot,
fitted best to furnish breakfasts forth
along with your companions, chicken ova –
the tender and the tough together yoked.
But the seven species of wild hog and boars
are no such proleptic meals on trotters:
the wild boar of Europe, Asia, North Africa,
three hundred and fifty pounds of rending power,
sacred to Freya once at the winter solstice
(whence the English sucking-pig at Christmas),
the bristles painting many a fine picture:
the smaller crested soor of India
has been at times too much for even tigers
(not to mention luckless unhorsed sahibs):
the African river hog or bush pig
besouth Sahara, and its Madagascar cousin,
prefers a night life in the bush and forest:
the giant forest hog of Africa
was quite unknown till nineteen hundred and four,
so secretive its life in the deepest jungles:
that roaring extravert the wart-hog, with

Cromwellian warts and all, on the open plains
openly rootles among the grazing herds:
nor the pygmy hogs of the eastern Himalaya
standing barely a foot in height at the shoulder,
nor its larger cousin the Celebes babirusa
(that some are loth to grant the name of pig)
whose canine fangs stick up through its cheeks.

America has no indigenous swine,
only peccaries, killers of rattlesnakes:
but though they're no true pigs the peccaries
are swine enough for we non-specialist souls,
the two kinds (collared and white-lipped peccaries)
rootling in forests in large if loose-knit bands
from Texas down to Patagonia
behaving much the same as Old World pigs:
is there an ear so fine can tell apart
the tenor squeal of a stuck pig from a peccary's?

Who ever called the hippopotamus
a pig? Call the albatross a gull!
The hippo of the potamus a pig –
our river-horse classified with swine!
But so anatomists, who care no whit
for niceties that don't conform to truth,
affirm he is, this muckle blubber-bubble
surely invented (not mimicked) by Walt Disney,
an animated four-ton cartoon.
But the simple animal dignity of the beast,
that in primeval times did its dainty
underwater dance on the bed of Thames,
Humber and Severn, the Rhine and other rivers,
now but lives by human sufferance
in a few contracting parts of Africa!
That peg-toothed gaping maw may never be
seen by our grandsons but in picture-books,
unless, unless, unless ...
And the pygmy hippo of Liberia
and the forest rivers of Sierra Leone
is just as little likely to survive.

(63)

'Odd-toed ungulate' is surely
no way to describe that noble beast
the horse; but that's the name Science gives it,
The Greek sounds better – *perissodactyla.*
But the clan includes not only horses proper
but asses, zebras, tapirs, the rhinoceros.

The true king of beasts is not the lion
but the horse, his majesty the Arab stallion,
immense pride to immense meekness yoked,
romantic symbol of power, and of time:
the horseman riding the ridge of desert sand,
burnous and mane billowing and streaming,
the world of T. E. Lawrence and all that:
the aristocrats of sport, the steeplechasers,
the Derby winners, the thorobred Oaks fillies.
But more important are the humble workers,
the mighty Clydesdales and their fellow-drudges
from other airts, the unpaid labourers
of trade, the servant's servant, the man of wealth's
cheapest minion, mankind's greatest friend
by far, whose name's used still to measure power.
Yet horses are late-comers on the scene
of mankind's animal helpers, long preceded
by dogs and various domestic cattle,
first arriving as a chariot-puller,
then as the steed of the daring mounted rider
(the man-horse, centaur to the simple),
bringing with them social revolutions.
Man-sick Swift saw them as a higher order
and made his men subservient to horses;
Roy Campbell, tamer of horses and poems,
saw salvation in caballero countries,
the pre-industrial, 'civilised', horsey world;
while Edwin Muir, no anti-humanist,
saw them survive Man's racial suicide
to re-form on the Earth a natural order.

A history of the horse would prove to be

substantially a history of Man
from mythic times, when great Bellerophon
mounted the winged horse of inspiration,
to Alexander on Bucephalus
Macedonianising the known world;
Pharaoh's chariots' horses in Moses' time
drowned in the Red Sea; Mazeppa's ride;
the Tartar horde that swept across the Steppes
and laid the barbarous Russians under tribute
(with each conquering khan up in the saddle
came the real conqueror, the horse)
down to our own times and the prairie cowboy
fixed in the filmy myth, Tom Mix and Tony,
and that horsey intellectual, Clever Hans.

Anti-climactic now it seems to return
to the few wild horses still found here and there
in corners of the Earth – the Gobi desert
where the wild horse of Mongolia alone
survives, akin no doubt to the horse Timogen,
Kubla and other Khans rode, and all their horde
who swayed vast tracts of Earth from Karakoram:
the Central Asian deserts too still know
the hooves of the onager, chigetal and kiang
(those horses which have been misnamed 'wild asses'):
other 'wild' horses are domestic ferals.

Zebras, whose wild stallions Campbell has
rolling their mares among the trampled lilies,
are also under the sword of Damocles,
the mountain kind, or Greevy's rarer one
the bontequagga (kin of the extinct quagga)
all are doomed unless men undoom them –
these beautiful black-striped, white-furred animals,
and the true wild ass of north-east Africa
also lives on seemingly borrowed time.

Primitive survivors of a race long gone,
the tapirs cling to life as best they can:
the Malay tapir, patches of black and off-white,
plucking at twigs and branches and water plant-life,

the four American kinds a dingy brown
(dinginess sums up their looks and outlook)
roaming the South and Central American forests;
the common one, Daw's, Roulin's, and Baird's
(Roulin's browsing far up the Andes),
all plucking at life with stumpy trunk
or walking the river-beds in quest of plant-life:
strange variations played on the notochord,
yet Earth will be the poorer for their going.

I can't shake off the pessimistic cloud
broods on the contemplation of these mammals,
so many breasts poised upon extinction,
so much kindly milk for men to squander:
these nosehorns from the prehistoric ages
lumbering, living tanks, as much at home
in this atomic age as would be, say,
a dinosaur in Madison Square Gardens,
pathetic in their helpless belligerence,
myopic monsters in their armoured hides,
whether the plated giants of the Indian plains
or those that roam the African savannahs.
See a pack of wild Cape hunting-dogs
intent on making a baby-rhino meal,
how they dog and harass the mother and the calf,
one distracting the dam while another seizes
the squealing calf by the ears till she turns and charges,
clumsy as backing lorry, while junior tries
to huddle under her massive sides and can't.
No bull by muletta is so fuddled
as this poor beast in her long and foredoomed trial.
Soon the calf is bleeding at the neck,
the dogs employing picador techniques,
weakening the calf till nightfall comes
when they can all come tearing in for the kill,
terrible jaws rending belly and crotch –
Nature in the raw is bloody gruesome.

The great white rhino, biggest of them all,
South Africa's already done to death
and soon will die in other parts as well.

The black, the other two-horned African species,
will not be many years behind the white.
Will Hindu fellow-feeling for our kindred
spare the mighty one-horned Indian rhino
plated in his folds of armoured hide,
or its lesser cousin of the Javan forests,
or the smallest of these nosehorns in Sumatra?
Does Nature care a damn, either way?

(64)

The pundits, always ready to astound us,
place the little hyrax (tailless, earless
short-legged bunny-rabbit) in between
the rhinos and the mighty elephants –
a most unlikely setting for a coney.
There, however, mere bards must leave them
till Science finds some other place to put
the two kinds, the ground and the tree-climbing,
with their various species throughout Africa,
the middle-east and adjacent parts of Asia:
timid little vegetarian beasts,
the rock hyrax who lives in colonies
on rocky ground, like its larger big-toothed cousin,
and the solitary hyrax of the trees –
night-feeders on the topmost foliage.

(65)

The Life-artist in his serious play
has already played so many variations
on the theme of bony endoskeleton
you'd think there could be little left to do
but you'd be wrong – there is no limit,
and he who made the tiniest humming-bird
delights as much in the African elephant,
that great beast that seems made of tree –
four stout boles the legs, a hanging branch
the trunk, body the bole of some tree giant
cut off and shaped, bark and all, to serve
its turn, a twig the tail, the fanning ear
derived from mobile bark: truly it seems
the very spirit of tree in a beast incarnate,
a living god of trees, king of the forest,
the adults never (or rarely) lying down.
Yet, as I write, this god in Kenya alone
is being gunned to extinction so that a few
wicked rascals living above the law
can grab illusory wealth for crimes against Life.
If other elephant countries are as bad
(killing even babies for ivory)
this beast will join the dodo and the auk,
and his little forest brother of Sar Leone
before this murderous century's extinct.

Happy his lesser kin of India
too useful still as heavy labourer
to be abandoned to power-mad criminals
who don't just live above, but make, the law.
And wherever Hindu influence prevails
or that of the Enlightened One, Gautama,
reverence to common sense is added
to help preserve this patient, noble creature
from whom mankind benefits so much.
Its wisdom shows up in its way of sleeping –
four hours round noon, and four again round midnight,
properly relaxed in the horizontal,
and in how a mother gets a calfless girl-friend

to help preserve the baby from the tigers,
and how the herd protects the birthing mother
(calves are too rare for prodigal abandon):
the mother even carries the calf to safety.
No wonder it bears the world for many Asians.

Most fortunate of all the elephants
is one that lives in Sumatra – it has no tusks:
most unlucky, the tetrabelodon,
a four-tusker now of course extinct:
though Denis traced a dead one in the 'thirties,
rescuing the skull with all four tusks.

(66)

Nature favours the modest and the small
so mice will long outlive the elephant,
the vole the lion, the squirrel the grizzly bear,
as the sparrow shall outlive the golden eagle.
So these beasts who gnaw things for a living
shall long outlive our mightiest carnivores,
comparatively safe in holes and burrows,
lucky to have no commercial value
save for a few the fur-trade persecutes.
Far from being threatened with extinction
their numbers have to be controlled by men
whose riches rats and mice lay under tribute.

Transformers of dead wastes to fertile soil,
the rodents challenge Man's monopoly
and seizure of Earth's cornucopia,
the single-tooths by far the most successful –
squirrels, mice and voles and porcupines,
a vast and various, superabundant clan.

Skiuros, the shading-tail, alias squirrel,
delight of children here in parks and gardens
(Princes Street for instance among the traffic),
peanuts from small by smaller fingers taken
pert and perky, nervously bold, grey charmers
(tail a balancing rudder for aerial leaps)
and in the highlands, reds may still be seen.
But these are but two of a numerous family:
the scaly-tails or African 'flying' squirrels,
the West African giant and side-striped squirrels,
pygmy squirrels, the various African ground ones,
American chickarees, the Costa Rican,
the Indian giant, the great-eared of Borneo,
long-nosed squirrels of Burma, Siam and China,
the 'flying' squirrels of the Old World and the New,
the tufted-eared, the fox, the flame-squirrels,
their ground relatives of divers kinds –
marmots, chipmunks, prairie-dogs and sousliks,
spermophiles (pouched marmots), bobacs, woodchucks

antelope squirrels and the pocket gophers,
North American swellels and, above all,
that Daedalus of the species, the ingenious beaver
(builder of dams and lodges with trowel tail)
whose name's a password for the industrious:
all these beasts we humans find simpatico,
cuddly creatures exciting pleasant feelings.

Not so the rats and mice exciting hatred
and fear, rousing murderous impulses.
They gnaw at our flooring and other house timbers,
reive our food from larder and from field,
frighten the women – wherever we are,
rats and mice like our incarnate sins are,
inseparable from us as our shadows,
horrible creatures (pardon the psapphics).
Who but rats well into recent times
spread pestilence throughout whole continents
(the Black Death, bubonic plague and such),
enemies of mankind that still we're stuck with?
I love animals as much as most
but when my own are menaced I am man –
hand me that club and watch me at the killing,
murdering rats without a trace of mercy
just as medics murder our diseases.
If Man's survival made it imperative,
I'd end zoology – my kind, right or wrong.
Rats and their fleas and lice – what misery
they've caused and cause so many of mankind:
even to-day we hear of babies eaten,
old folk bitten in their dying beds!
Hand me that club, give me my working ferrets,
the rats are undermining my children's house,
the future of mankind is sabotaged,
give me that poison, hand me down that gun:
in killing rats, no way is a bad way.

But look, what's this? these little pocket mice,
that kangaroo rat are surely not for murder?
No, but they are neither mice nor rats
nor squirrels either, though close akin to both.

They are a link between the mice and squirrels,
living in arid, unlikely American places
where they never seem to drink, some of them
so small an ounce tips the scale against them,
these hetero-mice with fur-lined cheek-pouches,
the Life-artist's exquisite miniatures:
while kangaroo-rats, also American souls,
can leap the length of a man and more,
store several gallons of seed in sand burrows
and live lifelong with never a drop of water.
Lone-wolf individualists, if two
meet up, they kangaroo-box till one is dead.

And look, too, at this undoubted mouse
curled in its hibernation hole in a tree,
the squirrel-like dormouse, or the harvest-mouse
in its woven nest high up among the reeds:
are these, would you say, enemies of mankind?
The world is full of mice and rats that never
sabotage a house or spread a plague
or do any serious harm to lordly Man:
grasshopper mice and white-footed deer-mice,
scorpion mice that live on scorpions,
rice rats, cotton rats, Rocky Mountains wood-rats
hoarding seeds and nuts in its high-built castle,
fish-eating rats of South America,
yellow-necked mice that shun the light of day,
the multimammate mice with twenty teats,
roof rats, crested rats, bandicoot-rats and tree-mice,
grass rats, swamp rats, giant Gambia rats,
Australian rabbit-rats, and 'jerboas'
and all their prolific tribe of relatives –
jerboas proper, gerbils, voles and lemmings,
muskrats (benefactors of the fur trade).
They're a tribe that won't be easily extinguished,
and already we can see in some of these
beginnings of that greatest instrument
of adaptation yet achieved – the hand.

(67)

Porcupines, no spiny pigs despite
being so miscalled, but defensive rodents
rather overdoing it – no lovebirds they.
Yet crested porcupines (often forty-pounders)
will sleep in fives and sixes to one burrow
and the young come two or three to a single nest.
The brush-tails, long-tails, Asian porcupines
(though smaller) are no less with armour cumbered,
presenting life a prickly distrustingness:
and the various New World tree porcupines
can quell a lynx or puma with their quills.

They really are a sort of guinea-pigs
(themselves no pigs, nor even come from Guinea
for their home is in Guiana and such lands)
more properly called cavies (in the wild)
akin to various jumping hares (no hares)
of Africa, to rock-rats, gundis, cane-rats,
and even that mysterious beast, the coypu.
These tailless cavies (rarely a foot in length)
no South American country is without,
though the Patagonian maras are more like
the jumping hares, reaching three feet in length,
living in dozens in delvings in the ground:
and the stalwart capybara, largest of all
rodents weighing up to a hundred pounds),
peacefully browsing on Orinoco plant-life,
is little more than a guinea-pig overgrown.

In South America too that succulent beast
the agouti, and its kin the spotted paca
shaggy-rumped and tailless, bound and abound:
and in the Andes lives that 'terrible mouse'
the long-tailed pacarana (or false paca)
burrowing among the patient rocks –
unknown to man till eighteen seventy-three.
And that same rodent-blessed terrain
boasts also the incredible viscacha,
whisker-eyed with white-banded face,

a head too big for its body, a crested tail,
with (jackdawlike) a flair for collecting baubles.
They watched Charles Darwin watch them at their burrows.
There too, most beautiful of rodents
and most persecuted, the chinchilla
breeds for the furrier hundred-pelted coats,
pale silver blue as moon behind a mist,
its delicate fur finer than gossamer,
surviving only (widespread once) in Chile
high up in holes in rocks in the titan Andes
where Chilean laws endeavour to protect it.

West Indian islands, peaks of a sunken land,
alone produce the singular hutias,
last of a large and now but fossil race,
heavy, burly, coypu-like survivors
known to us for a hundred and fifty years.
But from the American mainland comes the coypu
(comes, for instance, to the Norfolk Broads
where some escapers make themselves at home),
the 'mouse-beaver', hunted for its pelt,
big as a goodsized cat or small dog,
its taste for vegetation here resented:
comes also the degu, and the sixty tuco-tucos.

(68)

Closely akin to rodents, double-incisored,
the rabbits, hares and picas of various places
among mankind's most loved, most hunted creatures,
indigenous to all parts of our planet
(except Australia and, oddly, Madagascar)
are the gentlest and most peaceable of beasts
though preyed upon by some of the most ferocious.
Too big for burrowing, the hardy hares
lie and breed in open forms and nests
even in Arctic cold and treeless heights –
the Arctic hare with winter and summer coats,
the mountain hare (or blue) here in the highlands,
hispid hares, rough-coated, of the Himalayas,
the prairie hares (jack-rabbits) of the Rockies
and their elsewhere cousins, snowshoe rabbits,
the common brown hare sparring in mad March.
The twenty-eight or so kinds African hares
meet other hardships on the open ground
(though the red hare lives in barricaded dens).

Neither hare nor rabbit but in between the two
the little cotton-tail of America,
though favourite prey of many predators,
is ruthless death for any luckless snake
happens across it in the scrubby brush.
Rabbits proper, borrowing underground,
make warrens also in human nurseries:
all too well known, hated as well as loved;
by myxomatosis hunted, not only by weasels.

But few among us know much of the pica,
six-inch rabbitlike beast (except the ears
hind-legs, and taillessness), mountaineer
of the Urals and the Rockies, in this at least
more like chinchillas: it harvests hay
(dried in the sun) against the starving winter.

(69)

If monkeys are the first cousins of Man,
dogs and cats surely are his second
(bitches and queens are HER second cousins, rather,
for mammals are the tribe of the goddess Breast):
with other highly intelligent carnivores,
armed with big canine and carnassial teeth,
we've come a long, hard road from the amoeba.

So lioness is queen of animals,
the best breast in the business, nurturing
five hundred pounds or so of her shaggy consort,
living it up on zebra, gnu and kudu,
royal game to suit a regal pride:
and where such beasts in Africa are found
you'll find the lion, under threat of extinction
from its only enemy, regicidal Man.
Already in Asia this dynasty has set,
though still a few survive in parts of India,
Persia, and the lands of the Two Rivers.
The days of royalty have long been over,
though some we must conserve for kindred sake.

Anyway, is the tigress less a queen,
her mate less regal and majestic?
Siberian tigers can outweigh the lions.
A tiger and a lion by mistake
came one day together in one zoo cage:
in one minute the lion was disembowelled.
Lions are known to steal hyaenas' kill
and sleeping is their favourite occupation.
No tiger burned bright in any forest
but lurked unseen under its camouflage,
though Blake was right about the symmetry:
evolution's the forge hir brain was in
and the Life-artist's was the hand and eye
that framed it, and more frightful forms by far.
And whereas the lion kills but what it needs,
tigers in Roman massacre may indulge.

All such mammalian souls are so akin
to us, we're everywhere among familiars,
totems, human analogues and types
too commonplace to stretch imagination,
denizens of the collective soul,
too homely for a poetry of wonder.
Yet miracles of living art they are:
the leopard found in so many habitats
(weird Madagascar has no cats at all)
in many varieties of shape and size
from Somali dwarfs up to the so-called panthers,
clouded leopards, ounces (or snow-leopards)
cheetahs, the fastest animals on land
(though really a genus on their own),
Siberian leopards, and the New World jaguar,
the black panthers of Ethiopia
(more dangerous to man than the normal lion),
cougars or pumas (American mountain lions),
caracals and lynxes, the lesser cats
like our wild cat of Scotland, Europe, Asia:
jungle cats, the fettered cats of Egypt,
kaffir-cats, sebalas (the black-footed),
America's ocelot in its gloomy jungles,
the serval of the African lakes and rivers,
cats, cats, cats – fishing cats,
fruit-eating cats of south-east Asia,
marbled cats and golden, spotted cats
and desert, manul cats of lost Tibet,
yaguarundis (otter-cats) margays,
Andean cats, tiger and pampas cats –
such a tribe of springers are our pussies.

Civet cats, genets and mongooses
are beasts that seem half weasel and half cat
and something indefinably themselves:
zabad, the Arabs call the civet stink
spooned from its pouch to make seductive scent.
Women leave no sex-stink of their own
and a large industry has to make for them
what even the lowliest bitch leaves in her piddle:
the rarest perfume pimps for the smell of cunt.

But these exploited beasts when in the wild
serve a greater purpose, spreading forest
by shitting seeds of trees and plants whose fruit,
as well as flesh, these carnivores devour,
creatures of the night that keep in touch by scent,
in Madagascar, Africa, various kinds,
in India and other parts of Asia:
binturongs of Assam and the East Indies,
fish-eating water and otter civets,
palm civets living mainly on fruit.
So the genets go prowling through the night
feeding on jungle rats and mice and reptiles,
some like little leopards, others tigers,
their cousin linsangs (banded and spotted) and
found throughout much the same environs,
partly all tree livers, partly ground.

Kipling's made the mongoose a nursery beast
through Riki-tiki-tavi, killer of cobras;
though its normal diet is less dangerous,
a hungry mongoose certainly kills and eats
poisonous snakes, poison-sacs and all.
The common mongoose (found also in Spain)
the Indian and African mongooses,
crab-eating ones, Africa's grey ichneumon
(revered by the Pharaohs, crocodile-egg-eating)
the white-tailed, marsh, zebra and dwarf mongooses,
the cusimanses and the hemingales,
the suricates or meerkats of South Africa,
are as hard on snakes as prophets are on sins.

Catless Madagascar has its fossa
instead (and having it, needs no other):
it's the link between the cats and civets
and said to be ferocious as the lynxes.

The aardwolf and hyaena come between
the cats and dogs proper (though the experts
range them both unlikely with the cats).
These much-defamed pack-animals in fact
often do their own killing (and

at times are robbed of their prey by skulking lions),
champing the biggest bones with grinding molars,
each pack almost feudal in its order
ranked under a queen of despotic power
marking off her territorial claim:
attentive parents (to their own kits at least
though all adults disgorge to kits on demand),
co-operative in their hunting work,
male and female hard to tell apart,
sleeping and breeding underground in dens.

Spotted hyaenas of Africa the largest,
striped ones lesser (also found in Asia):
the South African brown completes the tale:
for the aardwolves, though they look like small hyaenas,
are a maned or crested family apart,
living (as their name says) in dens and earths
like hyaenas, foxes and many other beasts;
creatures of a mild nightmarishness.

(70)

Dogs with wolves and jackals interbreed
but with cats or foxes never: thus defined
a dog is what he feels impelled to mate,
a bitch is what she will be mated by.
The grey wolf and the red wolf, both good parents
born to lead a life of Spartan harshness,
the Abyssinian wolf or cuberow,
the coyote howling to the moon above
the drear prairies, none are as bad as painted:
mating for life or at least till death do part,
father the earner while the pups are small.
Yellow-dog dingo, the one Aussie carnivore
(stone-age man's domestic dog gone wild?)
an outlaw clearly marked down for extinction;
the Indian dholes whose packs bring down the sambar,
Cape hunting dogs, the terror of bush and veld
(like hyaenas organised in matrial packs)
mostly living (as dogs do) on the run
settling long enough only to rear the pups;
and the various kinds of smart-alec jackals
(black-backed, silver, golden, Himalayan
Egyptian, Indian and side-striped jackals)
swift, intelligent souls, are also libelled.

Foxes, seemingly dogs, are set apart,
secretive beasts, unsociable, solitary,
traditionally brainy, amoral types
('Hugh MacDiarmid' means Red, son of Fox)
celebrated throughout our literature
for similar traits to wily Ulysses,
though rarely allowed, like him, to come off best.
The animal vision throughout literature
(Reynard the Fox for instance) sees men as beasts
or animals in terms of human beings –
a rich and valid field of poetry:
but I here try to see each as itself,
men and animals equal in being souls
akin in truth, not by analogy
free of the past's ignorant patronising.

Animals do not SEEM our kin, they ARE
(as Latin calls them 'beings-with-soul' in fact),
all akin as animated beings.
Most hunted of the beasts, the red fox
keeps down insects, rabbits, mice and rats,
one of the benefactors of mankind:
the Arctic fox can live where no tree can,
storing a larder for the famished winter,
scavenging leavings, at times, of polar bears,
hardy as huskies in that frozen waste,
his pelt too much beloved of heartless women.

The North American grey fox is unique
in climbing trees to shake off enemies
and therefore where no trees are you don't find him.
Many related kinds are still surviving —
desert foxes (the kit fox and the swift)
long-eared foxes, fennecs of Sahara,
corsac and Simenian foxes, chillas
or pampa foxes, and the large savannah,
various fox-like dogs, the red-maned wolf,
the bush dog and the Antarctic 'wolf'
so tame that Darwin killed one with his hammer
(thereby proving the ascendancy of Man)
like the culpeo (translate 'trusting fool')
and other sub-varieties and species.

Love a man, love his alter ego,
and the totem world which wisely kept alive
the consciousness of man and animal kinship
still survives among domestic pets
to-day, as in the Egypt of Anubis,
Seth, Thoth (ibis) and other animal gods:
and the Sphinx is woman-lion in one body.
We need the ancient wisdom of the Nile,
the divinity of animals and Nature,
and the wisdom of St. Francis and St. Bernard
who both saw that this humanimal
is but primus inter pares among beasts.

(71)

Biggest of carnivores (and least carnivorous)
lumber the bears bulkily down the hill
towards that final sleep, the grizzlies leading,
Bee-wolf (the Beowulf poet called him)
who honey, fruit and vegetables, even grass
(grazed like a cow) feeds on more than flesh
of salmon (in season), woodsquirrels and such.
The brown bears and the kodiak (largest of all
at ten or more feet, fourteen hundred pounds)
are mild enough, these great Canadian bears,
unless provoked, scavenging spawned salmon,
the male a loner, mother and cubs a unit
(as with most bears) into adolescence.
Lesser brown bears, the European, Crowther's,
Eurasian bears and the Siberian,
Malayan honey bear (the smallest of all)
the Syrian brown and the Manchurian grizzly,
so many kinds of closely similar patterns,
all tend to vegetarianism –
a trend that's growing too among the humans.

Black bears of America, the declining
grizzly chief among them, smaller than
the mighty kodiak brown of the north-west,
the shy black bear proper, confirmed tree climber
and many related species including bears
by no means black – the cinnamon bear,
the white bear of British Columbian isles
and the small blue bear of Southern Alaska,
some with markings like the spectacled bear
of the Andes foothills, and the moon bear with its crescent -
how long will they be spared upon the Tree?

Most beautiful, strange and far-out of these bears
is the Arctic polar bear, rivalling
the kodiak in poundage, truly carnivorous
feeding on seals, birds, walrus pups,
foxes, caribou when it can get them
by stealthy stalking over the tundra ice,

its yellow-white coat perfect camouflage,
the young born (bear-wise) in hibernation
(never deep) in a den of ice and snow
in Arctic winter's near-to-endless night,
less or more snug than iglooed eskimos.

The aswal (so-called sloth bear) of Ceylon
and southern India suggests a link
with the Life-artist's next line in creation –
pandas, racoons, kinkajous and coatis –
longer of tail, and the weight of a big man:
no sloth at running, and a sturdy fighter.
But can it win the fight against extinction?

(72)

Those aboriginal Americans,
the racoons, are most noteworthy not for tails,
fur, habits, or other notable things
but for their hands: a fact makes nonsense
of their name 'pre-dog' (*Procyonidae*).
Pre-monkey if you like, or pre-primate,
but the hand makes them decidedly post-dog.
So the racoon's long fingers reach out for
not only the salamanders, crayfish, mussels
and other food this waterside creature eats,
but for fruit, berries, the twigs of trees it climbs:
and from the hand of tree-climbers comes
the brain that guides the hand to shape the tools
that build civilizations, cultures, make
Michelangelo possible, and Bach.
Delicate-fingered coons that wash their food,
hibernate in winter in some den,
wake in spring to win (and desert) a mate
(as bears do), leaving her to raise the young,
decoying enemies on wild-goose chases.

Akin are the ring-tailed cats or cacomistles
(so named by the Aztecs long ago)
agile in pursuit of rats and chipmunks;
the coatis (as the Tupi Indians call them)
long-nosed twilight hunters of edible anything;
the kinkajou with her prehensile tail
(perfectly adapted for tree-living)
and her cousin the olingo of Ecuador
whose bushy tail is no use for grasping.

Pêre David (of the Peking garden stag)
came across in eighteen sixty-nine
the giant panda of the bamboo forests
of Tibet, and mountainous Sze-Chuan,
its black and white concoction said to be
good camouflage in tree-shadowed snow.
Mistaken for a bear, this six-foot beast
in fact is of the family racoon,

its hands less dexterous (but no bear paws),
a shy, indeed a fey beast in the wild
yet breeding only there: it must consume
some forty pounds of bamboo every day.

The lesser panda or cat-bear (cat in size)
is more bear-like in habits; chestnut-coloured,
with ringed and bushy tail like the racoon,
it haunts the forests of the Himalayas:
both these carnivores are vegetarians!

(73)

The rodents of all mammals challenge most
Man's assumed supremacy on Earth,
and Man's allies against them are the weasels,
ferocious beasts who kill for lust of killing,
stocking larders with dead or half-dead prey
for future use: common weasels, stoats
whose pituitaries, as light declines in winter,
stop the pigment flow, so coats turn white,
changing again as light returns with spring
(unless they live where there's no winter snow):
long-tailed weasels of the Americas,
pygmy weasels, Siberian kolinskies
(often known as China or yellow mink),
and many variant species the world over.
True mink also harasses the rodents
but is as fond of trout as mice and musk-rats,
whether in America, Europe or Asia.
The larger sea-mink known on the coast of Maine
has been extinct this hundred years and more,
while polecats and the ferrets were conserved
by men to use for rabitting and ratting
(and that since Roman times).
Strangest of all such beasts is the marbled polecat,
native to the Gobi and the Steppes –
a deep red-brown, splashed with dots and dashes.

Some of these beasts of course the furrier
has harassed and depleted, and still does:
the stoat for its winter (ermine) coat
and the kolinskies, while the martens and the sables
rank high among the trapper's favourite prey.
The Russian sable is the chief among them
but the beech, the pine, the yellow-throated marten
all have suffered: even that fighting terror
of North American forest-lands, the fisher,
said to kill even deer and put to flight
wolf and bear, and it eats racoons, lynxes
and porcupines (poison quills and all):
yet it's only a marten form, scarce twenty pounds.

The only thing fishers don't do is fish.
But they prowl about, swimming waterways
by night, these desperados of the cruel north.

Between these beasts and badgers are a few
creatures, mostly American, such as
the tayra or weasel-badger of Paraguay
and neighbouring places, a two-foot tree-climber
omnivorous of diet; the smaller grison
that burrows in the ground; the huron or qui-qui
of Chile and Argentina, used by locals
to hunt chinchillas from their rocky dens:
the African muishond (or badger-striped zorilla)
seems to combine not only badger and weasel
but traits of the opossum and skunk as well,
destroying snakes and rodents, meeting foes
with jets of stinking fluid, then feigning dead.

But lord of all this clan's the wolverine,
the big boy, four-foot shaggy prowler,
notorious of appetite, in part
deserved, in part grossly exaggerated,
a terror putting puma and bear to flight,
stalking and felling sheep and caribou,
despite the fact it's very poor of sight
(shading eyes with paw to scan as we do:
like humans also subject to snow-blindness).
The eskimos discovered his unique worth
and trim their parkas with the wolverine fur,
for it alone can stand the extremes of cold
without freezing to hapless face and wrist.
But this tough hombre too is disappearing.

(74)

Brock the badger, set in his tunnelled sett
(whose persecutors gave to us a verb)
waits for the twilight hour beloved of thieves,
before waddling out on bandy legs
in search of beetles, hedgehogs, worms and rodents,
fruits and nuts and other vegetables,
powerful of claw and jaws and teeth,
widespread in places as in kinds:
badgers of Europe, Asia, America,
Siberia, Japan; the teledu
and sand badgers of Indian Ocean isles,
the ratels or honey-badgers of Africa
and related parts (partners of honey-guides)
breaking open hives of wild bees.

Hunted by beasts of hyper-sensitive nose,
what better for defence than foul discharge?
So the skunks (though not the skunks alone)
have perfected this chemical defence
firing several yards an evil fluid
not only stinks but burns the eyes and nose
of any would-be predator comes near:
a two-gun terror firing from the hip,
but loth to draw, in no way trigger-happy
or keen to hear the howls of its fouled assailant.
Yet, as with the civets, men can make
from this abomination perfume for women.
Secure as a gunman, he leisurely strolls by night
picking up beetles and other creepy-crawlies,
berries and such, wild bee grubs from hives,
holing up by day and for weeks in winter:
the various species all-American beasts.

Lutra lutra, the (not-so) common otter,
the joker in the pack, the weasel jester
pulsating, vivid life in mammal form
(the Life-artist in a holiday mood)
diving and swimming, rolling and tumbling over,
larking with fish and eels and terrapins,

tobogganing down slopes of sand or snow,
life triumphantly in life exulting –
but eating too, sometimes hungry and sometimes
hunted by men (with less innocent sport).
The otter's holt in the bank of a stream or loch
(with back as well as front door) is the home
of April twins whose primary voyages
into their world is on their mother's back:
they learn to swim when she dives and leaves them.
Varieties have many curious traits:
the clawless otter moving toward the hand,
like the giant African otter but more so;
the hairy-nosed otter of Sumatra
(the purpose of the hair's a bit obscure);
the Amazonian saro or giant otter
like its African kin five feet or more in length:
and many others in various parts and places.
But chief of all this clan I take to be
the great sea-otter, heaviest by far,
of Kamchatka and the American Pacific,
a beautiful beast who lives among the kelp,
eats there, nests there, mates there, rears there,
one of the most adventursome of souls,
floating on her back among the kelp
suckling her kit or breaking open shellfish
on a stone nestled on her chest or belly,
or simply enjoying life, pure being.
With only the grampus to be wary of,
she treated men at first with open friendship:
but they have brought her almost to extinction
(though now by international law protected).
She shuns Man as a more-than-grampus monster.

(75)

Life is not all progress, nor progress itself
a striding always forward: life moves
forward, sideways, backwards, twists and turns,
two steps forward, one step back, the Tree
has branches that reach down not up, the twigs
nearer the ground than the branches they're the ends of:
so in evolution are regressions,
deviations, twists in all directions,
some forms that, having reached the promised land,
take one look round, say 'no thanks', and turn back.
Many such already we have seen
after the long and painful struggle into
forms adapted for the life on land,
turn back to mother Ocean and a life
of buoyancy free from gravitation's burden,
revelling in her upbearing arms,
counting the land well lost for such pure being.
So the walruses and seals and all their tribe
revert from land to ocean, not so far
as the great pelagic whales, but mostly further
than even the great sea-otter dares to go.

Least lost to land of all this clan, sea-lions
still have ears like most land mammals
and so 'eared seals' are classified:
found in most oceans save the north Atlantic,
bolting their fish whole (like all the tribe)
lacking molars to grind food into pulp.
Among all seals the leopard seal alone
feeds on hot life, on penguins, gulls
and such, spewing up (like owls) the feathers.
The northern fur seals of Pribilof isles
prey on fish (and are preyed upon by men
because their fur's the best for furriers),
the bulls on the isles at breeding-time never
leaving their stance to feed, for months on end,
the calves born to a life of turbulence
(every one has to be taught to swim),
one in every two never maturing.

The Californian sea-lion, circus clown,
is much the same (but has a taste for squid),
as are South African Cape and southern fur seal,
and Steller's (or the northern) sea-lion, biggest
of all (twice the size and weight of others),
though the cows are barely half the size of bulls:
this gap in fact's endangering the species
for cows and calves are often killed or maimed
by rival bulls in their possession battles
(and human depredation needs controlling).
The Japanese sea-lion is now extinct:
but Australian and New Zealand still survive
as do other species up and down the seas
(the South American sea-wolf) but for how long?

And the true seals themselves, the earless ones
who've travelled further on the long road back
to life in ocean, the furless *phocidae*
(whose hide makes good leather but no fur coats),
are the belly-god of certain eskimos
whose way of life is founded on the seal
for whom they'll wait at air-holes in the ice
for days and weeks in sub-zero darkness.

But the enemy of the seal's the commercial hunter
slaughtering by thousands at a time,
and fishermen of course, the seal's rivals:
the Greenland seal, the common, the ringed, are all
plundered by that cruellest predator, Man,
whose history's a tale of atrocities
beneath the capabilities of brutes.
The grey seal round our coasts and rocky isles
(I've photographed them sunning on the Bass)
is also yearly culled and abused by fishers
(some were fined for atrocities this week),
righteously keen on keeping down the other
predators on marketable fish:
the bearded seal (a giant of the clan),
the elephant seal (largest of them all)
and his nearly extinct kin of the north and south
(protected by America and New Zealand),

so many kinds – the monk, the hooded,
the Baikal seal, the Ross, the bladder-nosed,
the ribbon, the crab-eating seal, the leopard
which preys on birds (and other seals),
Weddell seals with their appealing eyes,
so human; all have suffered more from Man
than other predators. Whatever reason
led these creatures to desert the land,
safety from humans wasn't one of them
for no living soul is safe from human evil.

Their next worst enemy's the killer-whale
who preys at will on even the huge walrus
whose great tusks can fend the polar-bears off
from their young, born in the Arctic night.
No more than half the size of elephant seals,
their tusks make them twice as dangerous,
even to the all-powerful killer-whale:
they're used, too, to dig up clams and such
from the ocean floor, crunching them shells and all,
later vomiting up the empty shells.
None of this finfoot kind have delicate guts,
for all keep many pounds of stones and pebbles
always in their stomachs, to help digestion.

(76)

The souls that are the nearest kin to Man
feed not so much on flesh but fruit and insects:
even the cobegos and colugos,
the so-called flying lemurs (which feed on leaves
and glide on leathery webs from tree to tree):
true insectivores, like solenodons
(West Indies relicts of a sunken land)
have highly strung and sensitive nervous systems:
various tenrecs of only Madagascar
where they serve as hedgehogs, moles, mice and shrews;
the otter-shrews (or potamogales,
'river-martens'), the golden African moles,
hedgehogs, moonrats and gymnures, the African
elephant shrew (rat-size with kangaroo legs)
and the shrews proper – red-toothed, pygmy, long-tailed,
water-shrews, the tiny cinereous shrew
of Canada (ferocious mite in battle
yet most hyper-sensitive of mammals)
heart palpating a thousand beats a minute,
the hero (or armoured) shrew of around the Congo
and the little Etruscan house shrew (smallest of mammals)
less than three inches long from tip to tail.
So sensitive, a number of the species,
they easily die of shock, don't survive
the cataclysm of even the gentlest capture:
long-nosed creatures, over-sensitised
for life in such a brute environment.

So with the various water-moles or desmans
of Russian waters, the so-called shrew moles
and the moles proper, powerful of claw
and sensitive of snout, so many kinds
in so many places, blind earth-tunnellers,
a vulnerable yet tenaceous clan,
unconscious benefactors of the soil.
Their forepaws, too, foreshadow the human hand.

(77)

Chiro, the hand in Greek, *Ptera* the wing,
gives us the bats, the beasts whose hands are wings:
but more and more the theme is now of hand
and the variations can be played upon it,
till hands themselves play themes and variations,
flying not through the night but over keyboards.

Fingers webbed like queer umbrella struts
flittering-fluttering through the twilight air
like clumsier swallows after flies and midges,
more like clockwork models of wire and fabric
(liable to run down any moment)
they seem, try-out roughs for swifts and swallows:
seeing's deceiving, for in their sphere of flight
with sonar gear perfect for midnight flying,
no birds can equal their expert performance.
Yet I have known them hit my rod when fishing
deep in late night pool for trout or sea-trout –
our pipistrelle (or common brown) in flight.

Hundreds of species of bat, beyond my telling,
abound – small bats eating insects, large
ones fruit, long-tongued pollen eaters,
bats that swoop on fish in tropical waters,
vampires eating nothing else but blood.
In Lagos, as the twilight hour set it,
I've seen the fruit bats (big as crows) emerge
to caw and cangle above the feathery palms
like clockwork rooks, as the cricket orchestra
was tuning up for the long night's performance,
and along the Marina, towards the creek
with its mangrove swamps that open out onto
the Lago di Korama ('K'rama Water')
and the peerless casuarinas of Victoria Beach
(beautiful sentinels, best seen from the sea).

A breed of bats includes the flying-foxes,
rousette bats, hammer-heads and barebacks,
the New World javelin and flat-faced fruit-bat,

the great false-vampire bat (haunter of churches)
ugly as sin (except to the innocent eye),
it might have been model for Dracula
save that it's as harmless as it's frighful:
the house-building yellow-eared and little fruit-bats
and many others. The real vampire bats
(unknown in Europe where was born the myth
of human vampires, close-linked with the gentry)
are as small as they are dangerous to cattle
and other beasts, and even to sleeping men.
Scientists, for this, trap a few,
smear them with lethal germs and set them free
to reach their caves, thus destroying thousands
of these bloodlappers and disease-transmitters.
Human vampires need a different treatment.

The insect-eaters are a numerous clan
invaluable in controlling creatures
far the most prolific of land species:
sac-winged bats (sexual perfume-pouches
in their wing-membranes), sheath-tailed bats
of Asia and Madagascar, tomb and ghost bats,
butterfly bats, jackass, mouse-eared bats,
serotine and silver-haired and whiskered,
noctule bats, pipistrelle, red, and long-eared,
free-tailed bats (or guano), crested bats,
naked bats and massive mastiff bats,
leaf-nosed bats and horseshoe – vast the clan
of these mammalian miracles in flight.
Rarer kinds like ospreys stoop on fish,
or live on flesh like any carnivore:
some, the cannibals, prey on other bats.

(78)

But more and more this bony skeleton
from fins and feet evolves the mighty hand,
greatest yet of tools of adaptation:
the little tree-shrew, seemingly half-squirrel
and half-monkey, uses its hands to eat,
and then to wash its face, now believed
to be the first of primates – that's to say
the hand-users, including manual man.

The tree's the cause that made the primates prime
for life in trees necessitates the hand,
and the fact that trees are areas of air
scribbled through with connected bits of land
almost like stepping-stones across a river,
precarious holds for hands, with death between,
security entirely self-dependent
and each mistake likely to be fatal
(no mere trivial stumble as on ground),
a premium is put on sight and judgment
(you cannot sniff your way from branch to branch).
Judgments of distance, weights, and springiness,
of dead and living branches, lurking foes
(and the higher you go the further the fall, the thinner
the ribs of land your life depends upon),
effects of wind and rain and other matters:
all these develop brain, alert perception,
swift and accurate decision, correct
perception of complex relations, right
and speedy action, steely nerve and sinew,
bright intelligence and understanding.
If Ocean mothered our bodies (and she did)
our brains, our minds, were mothered by the Tree.

Spectral lemurs, mostly of Madagascar
and nearby islands, vegetarians mainly,
gentle and timid creatures of silky habit,
slender of limb and delicate of hand
with vacant saucer eyes, limpid and tender,
most of them living the life of tree-dwellers:

true lemur, ruffed, fat-tailed and mouse lemur,
the ring-tailed living not in trees but rocks,
woolly lemurs such as the avahi,
the safaka, monkeylike indri or babakoto
(largest of all, and probably best-known).

Closely related, the mysterious little ay-ay
(so-called after its world-weary cry)
with spidery fingers for cleeking insects out,
combing its hair, washing its face, and drinking.
Slow and sedate, the slender loris moves
in the slumberous heat of Ceylonese environs,
tender-eyed as Leah, as Rachel beautiful,
with hands well-formed and small round ears,
a creature of the lower branches, unambitious,
snuggling contented in her brown fur coat;
but oiled lightning compared with her own cousin
the slow loris, for whom sleep's exertion.

So with their kin, the others of this clan,
pottas, bush-babies or galagos, the first
with spine half through the skin as defensive weapon,
a kind of mammalian happax legomenon
with a grip for its size disgraces a Herakles:
the owl-eyed tarsier is no laggard,
lithely leaping from branch to leafy branch,
with long ankle-bones, in pursuit of insects
in the jungle night of Celebes or Sumatra;
not the least wondrous in this world of wonders.

(79)

The man-like monkeys, New World anthropoids,
among our own first cousins our next of kin,
flat-nosed and smaller than the Old World species
denizens of the Amazonian jungles
and other of the South American forests,
nimble, agile creatures, highly strung
and tuned, with all-perceiving eyes alert,
judgment quick on the trigger, with no shadow
falling between perception and response,
no Hamlet trap of conflicting loyalties
to puzzle the will and paralyse decision –
these are the wide boys, immediate and simple,
tricksy souls, perhaps, but without guile:
perhaps, like children, of such is the Kingdom of Heaven.

Douroukouli or mirikina, the only
night prowling monkey, lemurlike
with furry tail no use for grasping branches,
howls about the Brazilian midnight trees:
the titi monkey, his larger daylight cousin
Uakaris, orang-utanlike
(though a tenth the size) of high intelligence
and highly living in the topmost branches,
sakis gentle and timid, over-dependent
if tamed, but never likely to survive long
except wild in the steaming Amazon jungles:
aluattos or howler monkeys, biggest
of the New World man-apes (in no way the brightest)
their magnified growls audible two-three miles,
widely spread through the South Americas:
capuchin monkeys (beloved of organ-grinders)
brightest of the whole American clan,
small and springy with long prehensile tail:
squirrel monkeys and spider (amazing gymnasts)
swiftest athletes of them all, arms
longer than legs (a model for netball players),
tail a fifth and better hand for swinging
(but hands thumbless for hooking rather than grasping)
and the woolly monkeys, big balls of fur

with a monkey peeping out: how clumsy we are
compared with these gymnastic miracles.
Man is the imagining animal
and supreme manipulator, but in all else
not one but many animals excel him;
and all, unclothed, can better endure the weather.

Marmosets and tamarins have claws
instead of nails on hands and feet, and so
are only semi-monkeys really, little
cuddly creatures seemingly designed
more for the nursery than American forests:
yet that is where they batten on bananas,
too many species even to be mentioned,
the lion tamarin said to respond to pictures
of other animals, as if they were real –
astonishing intelligence if true.

In spite of all these forms of anthropoids
how strange it is the New World does not have
a single ape, baboon or chimpanzee
with whom the human race is closest linked.

(80)

More doglike in their gait, the Old World monkeys
yet are nearer Man in other things –
same number of teeth, similar noses,
social organization and pecking order,
tending more to come down from the trees
and live aground, more manlike in their hands.

Fifty species or so of the tough macaques,
intelligent and enquiring brutes, able
it is said, to learn to handle hammer and nails
and other simple tools, to perceive distinctions
of colour, kind, weight, shape and sound
better than lesser species. They forage in troops
from a few to over a hundred, some dominant male
or female bossing the others, guilty they say,
even of the original sin that brought
war and evil into the world, the sin
of cornering food and starving into submission
less aggressive and self-seeking mortals:
no worse, no better (pace Darwin) than others,
superior in nothing but rascality,
like any bullying gangster anywhere.
I call it sin, but here anticipate,
for Man alone invented good and evil
and none can sin who do not know they sin.
Yet evil exists, whether known or not
for evil is what tends to end the species,
and good is what promotes its better life.
The lemming's self-destruction is an evil
although the lemming does not know it is,
and countless species in biological time
have, witless, brought extinction on themselves.
You cannot sin and not know you're sinning,
but evil is, whether you know it or not.
So our bully macaque, playing God
(who freely gives to all what Earth produces)
threatens its whole species with extinction
although it has no consciousness of sinning:
and in the pecking order it need not be

a matter of the stronger and the weaker,
but matter of the more and less egotistic.
Yet one of these macaques, the rhesus monkey
has made its name in medicine, like Pasteur
or Harvey, in the special sphere of blood:
and another one, the Barbary Ape (no ape)
helps the English army keep Gibraltar.
Others of the breed are less distinguished
though the Japanese ape (again no ape) is famous
as the wise monkeys who see, hear, speak, no evil.
Other of these macaques are the lion-tailed,
the long-tailed, pig-tailed, toque, black or Celebes
(in local folk-lore famous for its wit).

Mangabeys of Africa, named from a town
in Madagascar (where they've never lived),
trooping through the West Coast forest tree-tops,
sooty, white-crowned, black and crested species,
all, like macaques and others, with cheek-pouches:
confirmed tree-dwellers, by no means over-common
as the guenons are (some eighty different species)
maras and vervets, talapoins and grivets,
osok, avembo, green and Diana monkeys,
red guenons who live in the savannahs
already well-adapted to the ground,
leaf-monkeys or langurs of India and
China, some at home in the Himalayas,
some, like the hanuman, are held sacred
and some, like the wanderoo, distinctly handsome:
guereza or colobus monkeys in
their bishops' robes, gentlest of African monkeys,
and strangest of all, the proboscis monkey
at ease in tree-tops of his Bornean jungles,
able to dive and swim the doggy paddle,
with nose like an elephant seal, for God knows what.

(81)

Greatest of monkeys and nearest man,
the tribes of baboons have come down from the trees
to re-occupy the long-forsaken ground:
all African, the northern hamadryas,
the southern chacma, gelada of the east,
living in packs of sometimes several hundred
ruled by despotic males of varying rank,
patriarchates with females merely chattels
(often killed in the wars the males fight for them)
passively accepting their slavish lot,
abused and beaten for trifles (often to death):
societies, indeed, of battered wives.
Omnivorous brutes of high intelligence
(though mainly vegetarian by habit)
long of face and sensitive of smell,
in some ways like a cross of wolves and monkeys,
still these souls hold their own: for how long?
Surviving in wide range of territory
and temperatures of heat and cold, weather
as various as Africa itself,
they use stones as hammers on coconuts:
so Marais saw them break the baobab nut
otherwise only man can prey upon,
dig deep holes in sand to reach water,
and use reason on various other problems
(the chacma seemingly the most advanced).
So they possess like us a two-tiered psyche:
the primal animal one (so-called unconscious,
so-called irrational and instinctive), and
a conscious one of rational adaptation
not to typical but specific problems;
a voluntary and involuntary,
an individual and a tribal, mind.
And in between, a half-way house, tradition –
the 'instincts' of the post-instinctual.

Here with these baboons we reach an end
and a beginning; biological evolution
by natural selection here is giving way
to mental evolution by social selection,

the young inheriting not patterns but a tool
of adaptation to many possible patterns:
for social choice, influenced by tradition,
that store-house of past choices and patterns
vastly extending current experience
as literature extends the individual mind
to include not one but many lives, times, places.
Thus the loss attendant on a gain
is modified, as is the gain itself,
the absoluteness of biological choice
becomes a relative *ad hoc* social one;
resilience, not rigidity becomes
the mark of intelligent (not instinctual) living.
Mother Nature loosens her control
of children growing up to rule themselves,
within the laws She must herself obey.

These baboons, heroes of evolution,
prepare the way for man the maker
(whose therefore debt to them's incalculable),
prying into every nook of Earth
and settling there, not so much adapting
to conditions as adapting them:
the Tree has many branches, twigs and leaves,
but its only fruit is the intelligent soul
in which all other souls are taken up,
fulfilled, and find (or should) their true Protector,
Man, the grateful heir of evolution.

In these baboons, as later on in Man,
natural selection births a species
rendering its mother obsolete,
or at least replaced by a greater mechanism
(as is the fate of mothers), intelligence.
Social selection replaces natural,
conscious (more or less) not instinctive:
specialisation, and its limiting ills
of unadaptability to change,
gives way to generalised ability,
not confined to a niche in a nook of a place
but world-wide, inheriting planet Earth.
Baboons beget citizens of the world.

(82)

Between these monkeys and Man, the great apes
of the forest hold their kingship of the trees:
the gibbons (those monogamous tree-walkers),
orang-utan (the old man of the woods)
that solitary of East Indian jungles,
the king-o-the-woods himself, the chimpanzee,
at home aground, yet master of the trees:
and the great gorilla, most at home aground
among the forest's densest undergrowth.

So at our Tree's highest peak we find
the forest tree that only God can make,
the alma mater of our primate soul
(therefore herself the soul of poetry),
the tree of the African forest, semi-deciduous,
shedding leaves in rotation (so evergreen)
in a sun-spoilt land of never-ending summer
vibrant with life, and loud with Van Gogh colours,
forests breathing out vast quantities
of the oxygen that makes our Earth alive
(alone of planets), trees with sunlight laced
and emphasised with angled shade and sunbeam.
There in that primeval silent stillness
heavy with the feel of Africa
(endlessly old and rich, eternally young),
trees growing in stalwart dignity,
unflappable massive calm, the universe
in microcosm, every leaf a sun
and every tree a countless galaxy
born of a seed that pushes up a shoot
that puts down roots, becomes a trunk,
branches out and sub-branches, twigs
and leafs and flowers, bears in season fruit,
alone and apart in contact with its fellows,
each a world for insects, birds and beasts,
the forest moths, butterflies and beetles,
a home for lianas and various flowering creepers,
shelter and cover for animals and plants,
feeding the soil with compost of dead leaves:

and in its time dies, and crashes down,
makes room for and feeds other forms of life.

Trees of more kinds than I can ever name
from the palm fringes to the deepest ironwoods,
trees from man-size saplings, bush and shrub,
to skyscraping giants, many-storied homes
for tropical creatures: those of the lowest branches,
those of the middle and upper, and the myriad life
lived in the topmost canopy, brassy flowers
and loud birds and butterflies, red-tailed monkeys,
cowled colobus, blue and other species,
hornbills, various kinds of snake, tree frogs,
lizards, touracous and rollers, doves.
Francolins and guinea-fowl on the ground
where the shy duiker is the favourite prey
of the many stronger species, where hog and bushbuck
run, and buffalo browse by the river edges
and even the mighty elephant may saunter:
bats and birds of prey above the canopy,
parrots and cuckoos, and the silent leopard prowls.

But the forest chiefly's the home of chimpanzee,
not travelling through the lofty canopy
but feeding on varieties of fruit
(mostly bitter) according to the season
(some rich and fattening, others lenten)
moving from tree to tree, mostly not swinging
but lolloping across the forest floor
on which they wear itinerary paths,
living the sinless life of Eve and Adam
mindlessly mouthing fruit in the garden of Eden.

These black apes, so unmistakably human,
live their so monotonous lives together
in easy-going troops and multi-families,
liberal societies, laissez-faire,
unlike the authoritarian baboons,
but little preyed upon, a mild existence –
for even the leopard chooses better fare.
They don't indulge in fratricidal battles

(whether for females or other rivalries),
nor bully-boy rackets like the feudal barons,
but rather like a humble peasantry
work their way around the natural year
(the stuff of Thalia, not Melpomene),
devoid of hubris, happy to raise a laugh:
devious rather than belligerent,
capable of friendship, tender parents,
sociable, gregarious to a fault,
susceptible of lonely melancholy,
yet mischievous as urchins in bazaars.

Like crowsnests in the towering canopy
or lower down almost to the ground,
these creatures weave the branches into nests
and there recline as if in hammocks,
relieved of the heavy strain of gravity
almost as if relieved of it in water,
and sleep through tropical nights of calm or storm,
their only fear the sudden fear of falling
(that still wakes humans many a night in bed
though we forget when last we slept in trees).
These creatures have a habit adumbrates
the African bush telegraph of drums
by which news can be sent a thousand miles
in record time (as the dawn of Ramadan
still is drummed from Katsina down to Lagos):
so these chimpanzees hold celebrations
called by drumming on ironwood buttresses,
excited gatherings of neighbour groups
to which the drums provide a background music.
Among the sounds the jungle can evoke
the calls and cries of birds and hyraxes,
monkey chatter, coughs and grunts and gurgles,
cawing of bats and hornbills, squawks of parrots,
and always the night-long cicada chorus,
the chest-booming of the male gorilla,
surely this is the most extraordinary.

Chimpanzees, like other animals,
have something like a sound vocabulary,

understood of course by them alone:
but early human language is a song
(as Yoruba depends on pitch for meaning,
a factor used in telegraphic drumming)
only later analysing into
phrases, and lastly, words: among these primates
we are never far from the simple human.
with these volatile creatures we are on
the very edge of human life – gorillas,
orang-utans, gibbons and siamangs
are less akin to us, and the first two
I cannot see survive the century
without great human effort in defence
of creatures we owe both respect and love,
for they – all apes – are clearly of our kind:
they begin the experiment of mind.

(83)

There the animal fable ends, except
that every end in life is a beginning
and where the zoa end, mankind begins,
begins six hundred thousand years ago,
so Science tells us, with arithmetic
so awesomely exact I marvel at it
as the last and greatest marvel of the world
(let any doubters count them for themselves);
but truly I believe but a day ago
compared with the year or so of other creatures.
We are Johnny-come-lastly on the Earth.

How define Man? Apes use stones
to break open nuts and such, like early men:
where almost nothing is for Anatomy
to make its grave pronouncements on, I posit
as mankind's unique identity
not the *use* of tools but creation of them,
however crude the sharpening or shaping.
Apes throw sticks, but do not sharpen them.
Wherever we find tools made for purpose
there we find Man the Maker, *homo faber*
the artisan, the practical intellectual
not 'sapiens', for Man was never wise
and 'homo sapiens' is vain pretence,
self-importance of sterile academics.
Man is the animal who fashions tools,
adapting his environment to himself,
and *homo faber* is his proper name:
Man the artist, half a million years
of age, give or take a hundred thousand.

How did he emerge? All is guesswork,
a field for poets rather than scientists;
the most important thing in life is play,
imagination's semi-idle games
of which most great inventions have been born.
These early men of Peking, Africa, Spain
and other parts, our own race and others

long extinct (or by our race extinguished)
would play with sticks and stones, flints and shells,
with the horns and tusks, the teeth and bones of beasts
and gradually learn an edge can cut,
a pointed stick or horn can stab, a bone
be used as club (a jawbone or a femur)
teeth and claws scratch and bite and tear,
horns be used for gouging, splitting, scraping,
chamois horns for hooks, hides for clothing,
tails for whisks, that reeds and creepers serve
as binders, ties, ropes, that striking stone
on stone sparks fire (from the bush fires learn
the attributes and power of fire), from lizards
leather, that feathers cover and keep out water.
On all sides Nature would be pressing
principles on all sides seen in use:
the weaving in nests of birds, suspension of
the spider's netted web, so many things.
And what amuses and delights in play
necessity may find a serious purpose for:
so children playing on a natural bridge
made of a tree fallen across a stream
learn to make such bridges of their own;
so caves teach the principles of housing.
Thus, for early man agog in his world
his mother Earth was also his schoolmistress,
and still to-day sophisticated science
learns all it knows at Mother Nature's knee.
We see such learning in baboons
and other creatures, although Man alone
can turn hir learning into making tools,
not *ad hoc*, but for general purposes,
the hand extended making for itself
the other animals' tools we swopped for hands.

So by forty thousand years ago,
or more or less, we find Man the artist
fully formed and flourishing, a hunter
and collector, domesticating dogs
as hunt companions, using spears and bows,
fish hooks and tridents, nets and traps,

clothes and houses, fire, crude axes, blades,
and painting marvellous pictures on rock walls:
to which Picasso played the humble student.

There biological evolution ends
with Man the Maker on his road established:
for what the Stone Age men were, so we are,
and social evolution then begins –
natural selection's despotism
by social selection's tyranny displaced.

(84)

Here then at our biological end
behold the Man (and better still the Woman),
the mighty hero of the hand and brain
from Nature wresting hir further evolution,
the human psyche in its human world.

But first behold that miracle, man's body,
product of countless years of evolution,
masterpiece of the skeleton of bone
the spine and skull, the jointed legs and arms,
the upright carriage balanced on the feet,
and most miraculous of all, the hand
of four fingers and opposable thumb.
With these weapons and their allied organs
Man holds such dominion on the Earth
as no other species known to us has held.
The engineering miracle of bone,
a few simple principles in action,
fleshed with its complex of muscled springs
encased in a sensitive and intricate skin
able to sweat, grow hairs, renew itself,
respond to stimuli through countless nerve-ends
integrated in a nervous system
centred in the marvellous human brain,
to endocrine network of glands allied,
fed by an advanced digestive system,
of arteries and veins and other blood vessels
pumped by a four-chambered central heart
oxygenated by a brace of lungs
and the respiration system of all primates,
reproducing by a sexual method,
division of labour geared to the utmost pleasure;
and all co-ordinated in a self,
a psycho-physical functioning unity,
a person countless millions years of age
with a tongue developing mouthings into speech,
bearing in hir mind as in hir body
a record of the whole of evolution,
pedigreed by this animal family-tree

of which heor's made, of which is the fulfilment (heor: he/or/she)
BEHOLD THE MAN! This is the miracle,
work of so many millions years of life-art
a bullet ends in a moment, ends forever,
and nuclear bombs can wipe out finally.
This, at its finest, Pilate, is what you
blasphemously nailed back on the Tree!
This is what you vile political gangsters
threaten to extinguish from the Earth,
and Earth itself, rather than give up
the abomination of your 'way of life',
so demonstrably now a way of death!

But we are mammals, animals with breasts
for suckling the generation to succeed us,
and Mankind is really Womankind,
the mother of the future of the species:
there's truth in the old joke that if all men
are sprung from apes, women sprang the furthest.
Indeed, Man's atrocious history suggests
that men and women come from different species;
warrior men from the fascist male baboon,
and gentle women from the chimpanzees.

BEHOLD THE WOMAN! goddess of love and beauty
incarnated in humanimal form,
uterus with a human being round it,
breasts with a human being in behind them.
Behold my love, the humble and divine
incarnation of her mother Nature,
Earth's daughter (in whom her mother's well pleased),
who would not spend the life of a single child
for all the causes men slay millions for.
If Man is war, the son of ruffian Ares,
Woman's peace, daughter of Aphrodite,
supreme achievement and living masterpiece
of the supreme creative artist – Life,
who worked hir way through evolution's ages
from protoplasm to cells to protozoa,
sponges, jellyfish and polyzoa,
lampshells, molluscs, worms and arthropods

on to the vertebrates, the sharks, the fishes
frogs and toads, the various kinds of reptile,
on to birds (those winged thoughts of God
teeming in the vastness of his mind)
the monotremes, marsupials, ungulates,
rodents, carnivores and insect-eaters,
bats and lemurs, monkeys, apes and men –
and so to the master-miracle, my love.

Behold her rising from her natal foam,
the protoplasm of shores unthinkably far,
the golden Aphrodite in glory riding
barebacked the white horses of the sea!
Those yellow cascades of her swirling hair
(for hands of child and lover twining in
during ten million years that formed our kind
in near-amphibious life in sea and river),
the clear eyes of her triumphant vision,
small nose with little use for smelling
(gates where spirit travels in and out),
the red lips for kissing, the little mouth
formed for moderate eating and for speech
(the flesh made word that is the fruit of the Tree)
the cheeks, the chin, the face of intelligent soul,
the little ears that hear undying music,
that column of neck which tulips up the head
contains the brain that governs all this beauty,
the perfect lines and volumes of her body
shoulders, arms, legs, the feet, the hands
that can transmit the lyric thoughts of Chopin
and many humbler, wifely manipulations,
carressing lover, soothing troubled child,
nursing sickness – the loving hands of woman.
See how those breasts proclaim her mammal triumph,
rearing globes of velvet milkiness
(the humankindness milk) those aureoles
pink and virgin, or brown with maternal function,
the stalwart nipples thrusting out for sucking,
the blue vein that down each mound meanders,
breasts of my love, Nature's maternal glory.
And how from there she tapers to the waist

and the goblet navel, then swells always out
and down and round, the belly an urn upturned
in reflection of the child-bearing womb,
plunging in a weir of maiden hair
over the glorious mount of Venus, down
plunging voluptuous round between the thighs,
the long tapering legs of my mobile love,
the river of the spine in its dorsal glen
splaying out in the sculptured globes of hips
with a deep and secret cleft lying between –
take all in all, a miracle of beauty.
And all as cleanly functional as machines.

There in that secret place between her thighs,
behind the apron of her reticence,
the longitudinal lips at love's touch open,
the magnolia sepals flood with invitation,
the hard penis enters and is welcomed
deep into the jubilant vagina,
up to where the yearning womb is waiting.
Pelvis on pelvis moving, clitoris thrilling
(like nipples on man, surely evidence
that we, like worms, were once hermaphrodite?)
and towards the orgasm ever mounting to
where we, at blast-off, into space go soaring,
leaving our Mother Earth, for a time, behind.
The impregnated seed in ocean growing
recapitulates our evolution
while the breasts with happy milk are swelling
and the belly's upturned urn goes on ballooning
till millions of years of labouring evolution
are spanned in the few hours of giving birth –
the waters burst, the fish becomes amphibian,
my love is opened out by the human brain
in its cranial case emerging, the egg-white cast,
the cord to ocean cut, the fish starts breathing
and a new mammal finds its nippled mamma,
functional beauty, a factory of milk.

But some can't bear the functioning of beauty
beauty alive and real as piss and shit

instead of abstract, dead, ideal as marble:
some find it hard to take that 'love has pitched
his mansion in the place of excrement',
that the lips of love hide also urethrae,
that vagina next to puckering anus opens,
that the Architect in joky mood has run
the sewage system through the playing fields.
But, Dante Alighieri, mighty poet,
master of the all-purpose singing line,
so it was with your darling Beatrice.
And Swift, who could not bear that Stella shit,
if he had been a little bit less mad,
had in his prayers thanked God and Nature for it.
The love that moves the Sun and the other stars
lives between a urethra and anus:
and the garden of the Earthly Paradise
is screened by hair between a woman's thighs.

As for her clothes, she is no fashion's puppet
trussed in knickers, tights and brassieres
but free as daylight in diaphanous veils
in no factory coloured but the soul.
Next her skin's the veil of faith in life,
and next to that, love of all living things,
a ministry of care for all that's living,
children of Mother Nature and her God.
Then she wears her hope for the human species,
maternal pride in all of human kind,
then veils of endurance, balance, mercy, wisdom,
of dignity, of cosmic sympathy,
of goodness, beauty, truth and holiness
round her cling. And all these hallowed robes
serve not to hide but to reveal her flesh,
enhancing it as arclamps do an object –
a picture, say, a castle or other building,
or spotlights glamourise a theatre star:
or as the Sun, striking through the forest,
clothes a tree in stereoscopic light
till the trunk, the branches, every twig and leaf,
flower and fruit, with energy vibrate
and, like the children of God, shout for joy.

BIOGRAPHICAL NOTE

Tom Scott, the son of a Clydeside boiler-maker, was born in Glasgow in 1918. The slump of 1931 brought the closure of the shipyard his father worked in and the family (he had a sister) moved to St. Andrews where his father worked in his father-in-law's one-man builder's business. After a year and a half at Madras College, where his literary bias strengthened, he left school and started work, first with a butcher, then in the building trade. St. Andrews, where he was befriended by Sir D'Arcy Wentworth Thompson, professor of zoology there, fed his lifelong interest in birds, beasts and fishes. The war interrupted his early studies as a singer and his beginnings as a writer. He served in Nigeria and then in London where he stayed after the war until the early fifties. In 1950 he was given an Atlantic Award in Literature and went to Italy and Sicily: later visits to the continent were to Belgium, Germany, Austria, Jugoslavia and Greece.

Edwin Muir invited him in 1952 to Newbattle Abbey College for working-men, for a year reading literature. He then moved to Edinburgh, went up late to the University and took his M.A. and Ph.D. there in English and Scottish literature. He has published several books of verse, criticism, one or two books for children, and has written the most comprehensive history of Scottish Literature yet done. He married Heather Fretwell in 1963 and has a son and two daughters.

The present poem first came to him in 1955 but, after one or two false starts, it was only in 1974 that it began to write itself.

The following have subscribed to the first edition of 'The Tree'

Mrs. Edith Bone, 1 Loanstone Cottages, Penicuik EH26 8PH

John L. Broom, 21A Franklin Rd., Stromness, Orkney

Professor P.H. Butter, Ashfield, Preston Rd., Bridge of Weir, Renfrewshire, PA11 3AW

Mrs. Mary D. Carrie, 22 Duddingston Park, Edinburgh EH15 1JX

William Cookson, AGENDA EDITIONS, 5 Cranbourne Court, Albert Bridge Rd., London SW11 4PE

Laurence Coupe, 72 Promenade, Southport

Robert Garioch, 4 Nelson St., Edinburgh 3

James Russell Grant, 255 Creighton Avenue, London L2

Michael Hamburger, Marsh Acres, Middleton, Saxmundham, Suffolk LP17 3NH, England

J.F. Hendry, 17 Ruskin Terrace, Glasgow G12

Jane Souhami Hogg, 5 Sciennes House Place, Edinburgh EH9 1NN

Neil & Rosie Hooper, 16 St. Vincent St., Edinburgh EH3 6SJ

T.S. Law, Blackwood Cottage, The Marlage, By Larkhall, Strathclyde

William Oxley, 6 The Mount, Furzeham, Brixham, S. Devon

Dr. Kathleen Raine, 47 Paulton's Square, London SW3

Professor R. Farnell, Dept. of Architecture, University of Berkely, California

Mrs. Goodsir Smith, 25 Drummond Place, Edinburgh.

J. Derrick McClure, 4 Rosehill Ter., Aberdeen AB2 2LF.

ISBN 9006135 00 1.

£2.60